EAT

EAT

EASY, AFFORDABLE, TASTY

FRANKIE CELENZA

Photographs by Lauren Volo

UNION SQUARE & CO.
NEW YORK

UNION SQUARE & CO. and the distinctive Union Square & Co. logo are trademarks of Sterling Publishing Co., Inc.

Union Square & Co., LLC, is a subsidiary of Sterling Publishing Co., Inc.

ISBN 978-1-4549-5591-7
ISBN 978-1-4549-5592-4 (e-book)

For information about custom editions, special sales, and premium purchases, please contact specialsales@unionsquareandco.com.

Printed in China

2 4 6 8 10 9 7 5 3 1

unionsquareandco.com

Editor: Amanda Englander
Designer: Renée Bollier
Photographer: Lauren Volo
Food Stylist: Monica Pierini
Prop Stylist: Maeve Sheridan
Project Editor: Ivy McFadden
Production Manager: Kevin Iwano
Copy Editor: Kerry Acker

Additional image credits:
Page 17: TCC Gallery/Shutterstock.com

To Heather
for always shining brightly

CONTENTS

INTRODUCTION 9
ABOUT THIS BOOK 13
ESSENTIAL GEAR 15
ESSENTIAL INGREDIENTS 19

23 SOUPS & SALADS
47 PASTA
67 BREAD & PIZZA
91 VEGETABLES & LEGUMES
115 BEEF & LAMB
135 POULTRY & PORK
157 FISH & SEAFOOD
177 DRINKS
199 SWEETS
223 SAUCES & SECRET WEAPONS

ACKNOWLEDGMENTS 235
INDEX 236

Boos Block

Introduction

Cooking comes with the territory.

My path toward cooking started one night freshman year when I was out to dinner at a New York City Italian restaurant with my friend Zack and our mothers. When it came time for his mom to order, she did so in fluent Italian, and then had a little bit of back-and-forth banter with the server. I was stunned—I had no idea she possessed this superpower! In an instant, something inside me ignited: I wanted to learn Italian! With a last name like Celenza and a love for eating, shouldn't I *at least* be able to order in the mother language of my ancestors? And so I began taking Italian, because I wanted to, not because I was told I had to, like the other languages I'd struggled to learn previously, most notably three painful years of Latin in high school. After a hard-earned C+ in my first semester, I felt the passion, but not the results. Fortunately, distant family in Italy invited me to spend that summer with them. I didn't know it yet, but the trajectory of my life was about to change.

Before that first trip to Italy at age eighteen, I had a whopping three dishes in my cooking repertoire: burgers, pizza (made with store-bought dough), and penne pomodoro. I did, however, have an appreciation for great homemade food because my mom cooked every meal for our family. Takeout was rare and frozen food was even less common (though I did love those frozen pretzels and the occasional TV dinner). When I was growing up, as soon as Mom called out, "Dinner is ready," my dad and my brother and I were expected to be at the table ASAP. I now understand why; cooking is an act of service, but mutual respect can be shown if the diners are at the table and ready to eat.

Needless to say, that first summer in Italy, I stood to learn a lot. I spent most of my time shopping with my uncle Andrea, eventually becoming his sous chef in the kitchen. Sure, I worked on my Italian, but the lessons came organically as he taught me how to cook. Andrea's dishes were stunningly simple, both in the way he prepared them and the ingredients he used, but he executed them effortlessly, seemingly improvising all along. And that's when I became obsessed with food—cooking it, enjoying it, talking about it, and planning the next meal (usually while eating).

When I got back to the States, and back to school, I started cooking in my dorm room. I'd invite friends and classmates over and churn out classic Italian dishes. They got a meal, and I was able to teach myself the basics: pizza, pasta, salads, steaks. It turned into a bimonthly social event—a dorm room dinner club, if you will—in which I'd managed to undercut our school's cafeteria meal price by one dollar. My kitchen faced outward, a natural stage that put me on display. As I fed my friends (and eventually newcomers who were truly coming for the food), I'd recount the myths and history of the evening's dishes, stories I'd learned in Italy. After a chorus of diners said, "Hey, Frankie, you should film this," I decided to go for it and in January 2009, I uploaded my first YouTube video, *How to make spaghetti and broccoli*. The response was small but encouraging. At the time on the few social sites that existed, there were almost no people my age sharing anything visual about cooking or eating, so I saw an opportunity.

My culinary path between that first YouTube video and this book is all over the place, and I couldn't have mapped it out if I tried. I started then stopped culinary school, only to complete the whole classic French curriculum online. I worked on the line at the New York City restaurant Lupa, with professional caterers, and as the private chef for the greatest male tennis player of all time during his 2019 and 2020 US Open forays. I've now hosted six different streaming cooking shows, including one hundred episodes of Tastemade's *Struggle Meals*, which showcases affordable, inventive dishes with humor, and now *Worth the Hype*, which allows me to travel and absorb knowledge from brilliant chefs all across the country. Even while filming these shows, the learning never stops, and I want to share all I've learned with you.

Some people feel like cooking is messy; you can cut yourself, or burn yourself, or ruin perfectly good ingredients by burning *them*, or scorching them, or neglecting them. But if you *want* to cook, if you have passion and put in the initial effort, it will become easy and, best of all, delicious. My goal is to ease the pressure for people of all ages and all abilities, and get everyone into the kitchen and cooking. If this book can be the start of or even just a small part of your own personal renaissance of cooking and eating, then I'll be a happy man.

About This Book

Expensive ingredients and difficult culinary techniques do not mean more delicious food. This is why I wrote this book, and its title, *EAT*, is also a promise:

- **Easy:** There are no hard steps to follow.
- **Approachable:** All the ingredients are readily available.
- **Tasty:** The combinations of ingredients make sense; you'll know this the second you take your first bite.

I want you to have fun, develop a food craving, and find a recipe to satiate it. I don't want you to head to a recipe with time constraints (only a few are long), or have any doubt of your ability to produce the final result. Cook for the love of cooking—it's the best way I know of to develop a skill that's truly useful for life. Simply cook the dishes that speak to you. Your uniqueness will continue your personal culinary journey from there.

The recipe chapters are organized into courses, just like a restaurant menu. If you crave pasta, vegetables, or sweets, simply head to that chapter and get cooking! Most of the recipes are written to serve four, so you can share the fruits of your labor with family or friends (or freeze the leftovers for future you).

If this is your first cookbook, rock on! Start by browsing through the first few nonrecipe chapters. This will set up your kitchen with the gear and ingredients needed to get started. You'll also get a few concepts and techniques that I think are useful to keep in your head. Finally, move on to making your first recipe. The easiest dishes are in the Soups & Salads, Pasta, and Vegetables & Legumes chapters. The hardest recipes to make (which are still easy) are within the Sweets and Bread & Pizza chapters; you'll understand why once you read the measurements section (see below).

Make the dishes, modify the ingredients as you see fit, scribble your notes in the margins, tell a friend, and eat together!

What Is Cooking?

Every summer when I cut into peak-juicy August tomatoes, I ask myself this question. Even when I pair those tomatoes with fresh mozzarella, extra-virgin olive oil, speck, basil, and flaky salt, I still ask myself, *What is cooking?* The reason is simple: When a dish comes together in 2 minutes and is perfect, it's easy to feel like you're beating the system. Like you should have had to do more to achieve this deliciousness. Don't allow yourself to feel this guilt. Keep it fun and keep it simple: Cooking is the act of gathering ingredients and preparing them. Sometimes heat is involved, sometimes not.

Then there's the cook (that's you!). Your finesse, skill, and intuition will all progress as you cook more and more. Before you know it, you'll reach the pinnacle of home cooking: the ability to improvise and adapt. In the recipes in this book, I've included sensory cues in addition to time cues to help give you a deeper understanding of what's going on as you're cooking. That's key to becoming the best cook you can be.

Measurements

Most American cookbooks use the imperial system of volumetric measures to express quantity. That's the status quo, and for that reason, I've stuck with cups, tablespoons, and ounces for the recipes in this book. You'll notice, though, that my baking recipes also include weight measurements in grams. Why? Because using a digital kitchen scale to measure by weight is faster, cleaner, and more precise every time than measuring by volume—facts are facts.

In these recipes, I've only given weight measures where I believe it's essential, and if a weight is given, that's always the preferred path to take, as weighing ingredients produces much more consistent results. A cup of flour can vary in weight by 20 percent, heavier or lighter, depending on the brand, the humidity in your kitchen, or even how it's scooped into the measuring cup. If you don't have a scale, baking by volume can produce good results if you measure correctly. Always spoon flour into the measuring cup, filling it until it's heaping over the top, then scrape the excess off the top in one motion using the handle of the spoon. This will give you a relatively precise cup measurement from brand to brand and season to season. Do not scoop the flour directly from the bag—doing so will compress the flour into the measuring cup, meaning you may end up using more flour than called for and your recipe might not work as intended.

When you do get yourself a digital scale, you'll see there's no turning back. Place a bowl on the scale, zero it out, then add your ingredient. If you're combining multiple ingredients, you can even zero out the scale between additions, keeping it all in one bowl. As a bonus, once you know how to use a scale, you can cook from any cookbook from anywhere in the world—and that's like taking a vacation without having to pass through TSA.

Always Salt to Taste

In this book, all the salt quantities should be taken with a grain of salt. Why? Because depending on the style and/or brand of salt you use, 1 tablespoon can weigh between 10 grams and 25 grams. If you're using a salt that's more densely packed and you measure by volume, you may end up adding way too much salt. The easiest solution to this dilemma is to first stick with a single brand of kosher salt (much better for grabbing with your fingers than table salt, and develops "salting muscle memory") to keep things consistent. And second, taste as you go. When in doubt, use less salt to start, then taste and add more as needed. It's that simple. Tasting as you go is an important habit to develop, so start now!

Building Flavors (Putting It All Together)

It would be so simple if every dish could have all its ingredients thrown into the pan at the same time. But if you want to build flavors, this isn't the way to go. A pan will always be hottest when it's empty, or nearly so. That's why most cooking starts with sautéing aromatics like onions, garlic, and ginger in nothing but oil or butter. Once that aromatic is browned, the high-heat cooking is usually stopped or slowed when the next ingredients are added to the pan. Here's a simple example for visualizing what I'm talking about.

Let's focus on three ingredients: butter, sliced onions, and tomato puree. To build flavor in layers, I'll melt the butter in a hot pan and let it brown a bit for added nuttiness. Once it's browned, I'll add the onions and toss them in that brown butter until they start to give off liquid, shrink, and intensify. When the onions are looking and smelling fantastic, I'll add the tomato puree. Being mostly water, the puree will instantly drop the pan temperature and will never again get hotter than the boiling point of water. This stops the onions and butter from browning any further. The flavor of this sauce will be complex as the sugars in the onions and the milk solids in the butter have both burned a little bit, intensifying and altering their flavors.

Now let's take the same three ingredients and place them all in the pan at the same time. What happens? The butter melts but never browns; the onions boil in the tomato puree instead of caramelizing; and the tomato puree is in control of everything because it's the dominant ingredient by mass. The order of operations makes a difference and is key in building flavors.

Essential Gear

My dad always says, "A poor craftsperson blames their tools." I prefer to put an optimistic spin on it: "With skills, you can cook any dish." But even though I love potatoes and steak cooked directly in a bed of coals, there's no way I know of to boil water without a pot, so we do need *some* tools. One more saying for you (this one from my friend Pete): "Chance favors the well prepared." While I think he was referring to rain jackets and tire repair kits for mountain biking, his quote is also applicable to cooking. But the key is to stay macro with it—you need some gear, but you don't need *all* the gear. Less is more, and if you're going to only have one of something, make it large so you aren't limited to cooking for one or two.

STOVETOP MUSTS (IN ORDER OF IMPORTANCE)

- Large stainless-steel skillet
- Large stainless-steel pot
- Large cast-iron skillet
- Enameled cast-iron Dutch oven
- Small nonstick skillet

OVEN MUSTS (IN ORDER OF IMPORTANCE)

- Baking sheet (even better if you have two) with a wire rack that fits inside
- 9 × 13-inch baking dish
- 9-inch springform pan (with 2½-inch-tall sides)

UTENSIL MUSTS

- Tongs
- Rubber spatula
- Wooden spoon
- Spider or large slotted spoon
- Tweezers

PREP MUSTS

- Large cutting board
- Stainless-steel mixing bowls
- Box grater
- Vegetable peeler (go for the Y style)
- Microplane (nice to have)
- Rotary grater (nice to have)
- Mortar and pestle (nice to have)
- Apron (don't ruin 352 shirts like me!)
- Dish towels/rags (you'll use them for everything)

BATTERY- AND WALL-POWERED MUSTS

- Instant-read thermometer
- Digital scale
- Immersion blender
- High-powered blender
- Food processor
- Stand mixer

KNIVES!

A chef's knife will be your knife for nearly all tasks, and is all you need to get started. One great knife is better than any boxed set of knives—don't be fooled into thinking more is better. Go to a knife shop, hold a few different models, and buy the one that fits like a glove. Keep it clean, and never put it in the dishwasher.

The Anatomy of a Knife

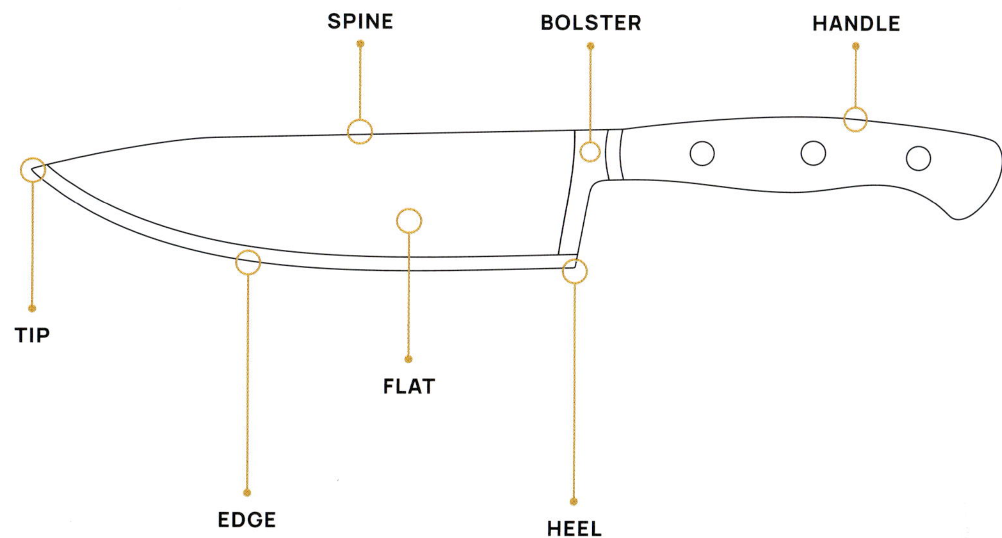

Knife Maintenance

Honing with a steel doesn't sharpen the edge, it merely maintains it. Hone your knife before every use and that sharp edge will last much longer. Even with honing, you'll still need an occasional sharpening. About every six months you can mail your knives into a sharpening service, drop them at a kitchen store, or get a whetstone and do it yourself. I do the latter, it's therapeutic and takes about 5 minutes per knife. Remember, a sharp knife is a safe knife.

How to Use It

Get a grip—for safety! With your dominant hand, grab the flat just in front of the bolster with your index finger and thumb. Pinch and hold here, then wrap your three remaining fingers around the handle.

Your nondominant hand is just as important. Hold the food with knuckles tucked and eventually practice having the flat of the knife in contact with the protruding knuckle. It's counterintuitive, but being in contact with the knife means knowing where the knife is, and that reduces the chances of cutting yourself.

1. The knife edge should always be perpendicular to the cutting board, a perfect 90 degrees. This protects you from slipping off angle.
2. Recoil: How high you lift the edge of the knife up from the board. The goal is to never go higher than the knuckle that's in contact with the flat.
3. Always ask yourself, "If I slip, will I cut myself?" The answer should always be no. If it's yes, change what you're doing before cutting.

SUB-ZERO
DUAL REFRIGERATION SYSTEM
650
GARLIC
PICKLES
S.PELLEGRINO
HEINZ
SWEET RELISH

Essential Ingredients

It's easy to think that a fancy gadget will produce better food, but great ingredients are the true path to flavor nirvana. Quality doesn't have to be expensive: The secret is seasonality. When you buy in-season produce, you're buying the ripest, highest-quality ingredients that probably haven't traveled far to get to you and that also are in enormous supply. Try to cook with the seasons—your food will taste better and cost less.

GARLIC

Keep heads of garlic in a dark, cool place, not in the fridge. To peel a clove, slice off the root end and the top, then press down against the clove with the flat of your knife to gently smash it, loosening the skin and making it easy to remove.

ONIONS

You must have at least two on hand at all times. Keep them in a cool, dry place. If a recipe uses just half an onion, store the remaining half in an airtight container in the fridge for up to 5 days (write today's date on it).

GINGER

Fresh ginger does well stored either at room temp or in the fridge. The best way to peel ginger is with a spoon, but you can also just wash the skin and leave it on, especially if you're grating the ginger.

CITRUS

Any time lemon juice and lime juice are called for in this book, they should be freshly squeezed. Luckily, whole lemons and limes can be kept in the fridge for about a month, making it an easy decision to pick some up, even if you don't have an immediate plan for using them. Lemons are a powerful brightening ingredient, and their zest and/or juice can be used in almost anything. If you buy them, use them. Do. Not. Fear.

PARMIGIANO REGGIANO

There are many impostors, and due to what amounts to ingredient intellectual property law, they are labeled as "parmesan." The real stuff is sold by the a block and has the words "Parmigiano Reggiano" stamped into the rind. Buy the real thing and keep it tightly wrapped in plastic in the fridge; it's cheaper than the pregrated stuff, keeps longer (I've never had Parm go bad; if you see tiny spots of mold, just scrape them off with a knife), and tastes better. It's worth noting that the rind is made of the same ingredients as the interior, just dried out. I like to freeze Parm rinds and pop them into soup for extra flavor—and to not waste a bit.

PECORINO ROMANO

This sheep's-milk cheese is much saltier and funkier than Parm and should be bought in block form for the same reasons. It can easily be substituted with Manchego, and can be used in place of Parmigiano, too—just use about two-thirds as much by weight, because of all that extra flavor.

BUTTER

Always use unsalted butter. It gives you more control of the salt level of your dish.

ANCHOVIES

These are a secret ingredient most people don't even know they love. I like to buy glass jars of oil-packed anchovies. I find these to be the most delicious—plus, I can reseal the jar and refrigerate them to use another day.

SPICES

I always try to buy single spices versus blends—and then use them to make my *own* blends. In general, I also like to buy whole spices versus ground because they hold more essential oils, which means when ground, they taste better. Don't be afraid of your supermarket's store-brand spices; they're often a great value.

SALT

Kosher salt is an essential. I exclusively use Diamond Crystal kosher salt, which is the least salty salt by volume. That means I have the most precision when cooking by feel. If you're using Morton's, cut all the salt volume measures by about half. For any other brands, it's a good idea to taste as you go and make adjustments. Flaky salt is also nice to keep on hand for finishing.

PEPPER

Freshly ground black pepper is an amazing spice. And it should always be that: ground from whole peppercorns right before you use it. Once ground, the pepper's aromas and oils will dissipate quickly.

GRANULATED GARLIC

I prefer granulated garlic over garlic powder simply because it retains its flavor much longer, thanks to having less exposed surface area.

OLIVE OIL

This is the best, tastiest cooking oil, and it's even better poured over basically anything as a finishing touch. I specifically mean extra-virgin olive oil, of which the best examples are fruity, sweet, a little bitter, and cloudy at the bottom of the bottle. Just plain "olive oil" is refined and often blended with seed oils to lower the price and raise the smoke point of the oil. Avoid this, and buy only extra-virgin. There are plenty of great brands out there—just keep trying them until you find an everyday olive oil you love. If you want to go above and beyond, search for a second bottle of EVOO that you reserve as a special finishing touch (just don't heat it; keep it raw). It's certainly not essential, but it's delightful to have.

NEUTRAL OIL

Grapeseed, peanut, safflower, soybean—these are my go-to neutral oils for baking, high-heat cooking, and dishes that don't benefit from the flavor of extra-virgin olive oil. You'll definitely want to have one of these on hand because they can stand up to a lot more heat than extra-virgin olive oil.

VINEGAR

Acidity is essential in cooking. It lightens and brightens rich dishes. It's also the only tool, other than dilution, that a cook can use to help fix something that's oversalted. Vinegars can be swapped pretty liberally. I like to have **balsamic vinegar** (nothing fancy, sweet, dark, tangy), **sherry vinegar** (like an oaky red wine vinegar with a delicious aroma), and **distilled white vinegar** (the neutral oil of vinegars; hyper versatile, including for cleaning!) on hand.

CALABRIAN CHILI PASTE

This chili paste used to be hard to find, but now I've seen it on both coasts and everywhere in between! I love the flavor and color it adds to any dish—it's spicy, acidic, and salty in a sort of lacto-fermented way, and the oily deep-red color is jaw-dropping. In a pinch, it can stand in for any fresh chili. I even like to use it like hot sauce! Keep it in your fridge. (Don't confuse this with jarred whole Calabrian chili peppers—they're not the same.)

MUSTARDS

If I could only have one, it would be Dijon. But my collection is larger than that, and includes spicy brown mustard, whole-grain mustard, and maple mustard (my favorite sub for honey mustard!). Mustards emulsify dressings, add viscosity to sauces, and help cut through richness everywhere.

WHITE WINE

There's always a screw-top bottle of dry white wine in my fridge. It lives there for one purpose: deglazing. (That's when you pour some liquid—in this case, wine!—into a pan after cooking other ingredients, then stir and scrape the bottom of the pan to pick up any little stuck-on bits, releasing their flavor back into your dish.) I try to find a $10 bottle. Deglazing with white wine adds a restaurant-quality, can't-quite-pin-down-why-this-is-so-great flavor.

BOUILLON PASTE

The easiest and most flavorful way to make a broth. Boxed broth tastes like trash, takes up a lot of space in your fridge, and only keeps for about a week after you open it. Homemade broth is king, but takes a lot of time to make and freezer real estate. Bouillon paste, like Better Than Bouillon, is the answer: Just mix it with hot water until it fully dissolves. Whenever I call for broth, this is the go-to.

A LOVE LETTER TO MOZZARELLA

There are three types of mozzarella: the shredded stuff that comes in a bag, which I'd like you to avoid from now on; the refrigerated fresh mozzarella sold in the dairy section of your supermarket that comes in a ball of either 8 or 16 ounces and has a sticker on it that says "fresh!"; and finally the *truly fresh* mozzarella. The *truly fresh* mozzarella is warm to the touch, sitting on the counter near the cash register of an Italian deli, cheese shop, or specialty shop. Someone there is making that cheese. Truly fresh mozzarella is one of life's greatest bites, and if you've never had it, run—don't walk—to the nearest place that makes it. It's not that one mozzarella is better than other, they both serve their own purpose. Once when I was buying *truly fresh* mozzarella from Di Palo's Fine Food in New York's Little Italy, co-owner Lou Di Palo told me, "Don't put this in the fridge because the whey will be absorbed into the milk fats and never return to its milky state." That milky state is what makes it so fantastic; when you slice *truly fresh* mozzarella, it leaks. This makes for a juicy mozzarella that's perfect on cold sandwiches, with summer's best tomatoes, and for snacking plain. Don't chill it, don't heat it, just consume it the day you buy it. The refrigerated fresh mozzarella melts fantastically and is great cubed up and mixed into warm dishes or sliced and broiled as a topping on sandwiches and casseroles. All the recipes in this book use refrigerated fresh mozzarella because the *truly fresh* stuff doesn't need a recipe. Just eat it.

SOUPS & SALADS

Spicy Coconut Tofu

Serves 4

If you love the balance of smooth, creamy coconut milk with a spicy, salty finish, then this dish is for you. Make it your own: Swap the tofu for chicken and poach it in the broth, increase the saltiness of the broth used, or add a little fish sauce. In a traditional Thai green curry, you'll find homemade curry pastes made with onions, hot chilies, garlic, ginger, lemongrass, makrut lime leaves, and more. For speed and ease, I rely on jarred, but this can be supplemented with fresh onion, ginger, and spices.

- 1 tablespoon neutral oil
- 2 green bell peppers, diced
- 1 medium yellow onion, diced
- ¼ teaspoon kosher salt, plus more as needed
- 1 (1-inch) piece fresh ginger, peeled and grated
- 2 tablespoons green curry paste
- 1 (13.5-ounce) can full-fat coconut milk
- ¼ teaspoon cayenne pepper
- 4 cups low-sodium vegetable broth or chicken broth
- 8 ounces pad Thai rice noodles
- 1 (14-ounce) package firm tofu, drained and cut into ½-inch cubes
- 1 bunch cilantro, torn (about 2 cups), for serving

1 In a large saucepan, heat the oil over medium-high heat. When the oil is shimmering, add the bell peppers, onion, and salt. Cook, stirring occasionally, until the onion just begins to sweat, about 2 minutes. Add the ginger and curry paste and cook until the vegetables have softened and are just beginning to brown, about 5 minutes.

2 Add the coconut milk and cayenne and stir well. Increase the heat to high. As soon as the coconut milk begins to boil, pour in the broth. Return the liquid to a boil, then reduce the heat to low and simmer for about 5 minutes.

3 Meanwhile, cook the rice noodles according to the package instructions, drain, and add them to the coconut broth.

4 Taste and adjust the seasoning as needed.

5 Divide the tofu and noodles among bowls. Ladle in the broth, top with the cilantro, and serve.

Cold Bell Pepper Soup

Serves 4

Gazpacho is a Spanish tomato-based soup, traditionally served cold. This bell pepper version is my spin on the dish. On a hot summer day, late in the afternoon, it's almost like an electrolyte drink in the fourth quarter—cool, hydrating, salty, light. Adding some diced ingredients gives this traditionally smooth dish a little texture and is a great way to hint at what's in the pureed soup base. I like mine at room temperature, but you can refrigerate it if you want an even cooler experience.

3 red bell peppers, quartered
1 pint cherry tomatoes
2 garlic cloves, smashed and peeled
¼ cup extra-virgin olive oil, plus more for drizzling
1 (2- to 3-inch-long) piece of baguette or other crusty bread, torn
1 tablespoon kosher salt, plus more as needed
2 heirloom tomatoes, coarsely chopped
½ English cucumber, coarsely chopped
Flaky salt
Freshy ground black pepper

1 In a high-powered blender, combine the bell peppers, cherry tomatoes, garlic, olive oil, bread, and salt and blend on low speed until smooth, 1 minute. Taste and adjust the salt as needed.

2 Divide the soup among four bowls. Top with the heirloom tomatoes, cucumber, flaky salt, plenty of black pepper, and a good drizzle of olive oil and serve.

Lentil & Beet Soup

Serves 4

This dish combines two of my favorites: quick, hearty lentil soup like Mom makes and elements of borscht, an Eastern European beet soup. Like most New Yorkers, I've enjoyed very delicious borscht with beef very late at night at Veselka, a Ukrainian restaurant in the East Village (I've even *cooked* borscht at Veselka with chef Olesia Lew). But now that I live outside the city, I have to get my late-night soup fix from my own kitchen. Lentils and grated beets make quick work of a dish that comes together in no time while instilling all the nostalgia.

- 2 tablespoons extra-virgin olive oil
- 3 carrots, thinly sliced
- 1 celery stalk, diced
- 1 yellow or red onion, diced
- 1 teaspoon freshly ground black pepper, plus more as needed
- ½ teaspoon kosher salt, plus more as needed
- ½ teaspoon onion powder
- ¼ teaspoon ground cumin
- 4 cups low-sodium vegetable broth or chicken broth
- 3 large red beets, peeled and grated on the large holes of a box grater
- 1½ cups dried red lentils
- 1 cup sauerkraut
- 1 bay leaf
- ½ cup full-fat sour cream, for serving
- ¼ cup chopped fresh parsley, for serving

1 In a large saucepan, heat the olive oil over medium heat. When the oil is shimmering, add the carrots, celery, onion, pepper, salt, onion powder, and cumin. Cook, stirring occasionally, until the onion just begins to take on color, about 8 minutes.

2 Add the broth, beets, lentils, ½ cup of the sauerkraut, and the bay leaf. Bring to a simmer, then reduce the heat to low, cover, and cook until the lentils have softened and are cooked through, about 25 minutes. Remove from the heat. Stir in the remaining ½ cup sauerkraut. Taste and adjust the seasoning as needed.

3 Divide the soup among bowls. Dollop with the sour cream, sprinkle with the parsley, and serve.

Pea Vichyssoise

Serves 4

Vichyssoise is a French-by-way-of-New-York-City potato-leek soup. The combination is great hot or cold; I serve it cold in the summer, and hot in the winter. The peas in my version are not traditional, but they lend the soup a beautiful pastel green color. Cooking the leeks very gently so they become sweeter but don't brown at all helps retain that delicate color. That's the secret: delicate treatment of ingredients for a perfect, simple start to a meal.

2 tablespoons unsalted butter
2 to 3 leeks, white and light green parts only, well rinsed and thinly sliced into half-moons (2 cups)
¼ teaspoon kosher salt, plus more as needed
⅛ teaspoon cayenne pepper
1 cup fresh or frozen green peas
1 medium to large russet potato (about 12 ounces), peeled and diced
4 cups Golden Rotisserie Liquid (page 39) or low-sodium chicken broth
½ cup heavy cream, sour cream, or crème fraîche
1 teaspoon freshly grated nutmeg

1 In a large Dutch oven, melt the butter over medium-high heat, then add the leeks, salt, and cayenne and cook, stirring, for about 2 minutes. Cover and cook until the leeks have softened, about 4 minutes. Uncover the pot, add the peas, and cook, stirring, until the peas are well coated in the butter and the leeks have completely softened, about 3 minutes more.

2 Add the potato, then pour in the broth. Increase the heat to high and bring to a boil, then reduce the heat to low, cover, and cook until the potatoes are falling apart, 10 to 12 minutes. Remove from the heat. Using an immersion blender, blend the soup directly in the pot until smooth. (Alternatively, carefully transfer the soup to a high-powered blender and blend on medium-low speed until smooth.) Stir in the cream. Taste and adjust the seasoning as needed.

3 If it's winter, divide the soup among bowls, garnish with the nutmeg, and serve hot; if it's summer, let the soup cool in the refrigerator for about an hour before garnishing and serving.

Tomato Bisque

WITH GRILLED CHEESE

Serves 6 to 8

This creamy, rich, and warming soup is so easy to make, and very nostalgic for me. As a kid, I remember walking through Central Park with mom to Sarabeth's, a restaurant that's still around today. Their tomato bisque planted itself in my head from the first spoonful, and all these years later I still remember its intensity. I believe pairing it with grilled cheese makes for the ultimate winter lunch or dinner. Try your very best to make a crispy not floppy grilled cheese that will dip into the bisque with structural integrity. Doing this is simple: Just keep a watchful eye on each batch, and use a heavy-bottomed cast-iron skillet for edge-to-edge browning. If grilled cheese isn't your jam, try the garlic croutons on page 37 instead.

For the Tomato Bisque

2 tablespoons unsalted butter
1 large yellow onion, diced
4 garlic cloves, chopped
1 teaspoon kosher salt
1 tablespoon tomato paste
½ teaspoon freshly ground black pepper
1 cup Golden Rotisserie Liquid (page 39) or low-sodium vegetable broth
1 (28-ounce) can whole peeled tomatoes, with their juices
1 cup heavy cream

For the Grilled Cheese Sandwiches

12 to 16 slices sourdough bread
6 to 8 teaspoons Dijon mustard
12 to 16 slices pepper Jack cheese
12 to 16 slices Muenster cheese
12 to 16 teaspoons mayonnaise
3 to 4 tablespoons unsalted butter

1 MAKE THE BISQUE: In a large pot, combine the butter, onion, garlic, and salt and cook over medium heat, stirring occasionally, until fragrant and just lightly golden, about 5 minutes. Add the tomato paste and pepper and cook, stirring, until the paste darkens, about 1 minute. Add broth and scrape up any browned bits from the bottom of the pan. Add the tomatoes and bring the soup to a simmer, stirring occasionally, about 5 minutes, then add the cream. Remove from the heat. Using an immersion blender, blend the soup directly in the pot until smooth. (Alternatively, carefully transfer the soup to a blender and blend on medium-low speed until smooth.) Keep warm.

2 MAKE THE SANDWICHES: Preheat the oven to 250°F.

3 On a clean work surface, lay out half the slices of bread. Spread 1 teaspoon of the mustard over each slice and top each with 2 slices of the pepper Jack and 2 slices of the Muenster. Place a second slice of bread on top of the cheese and spread 1 teaspoon of the mayo over the top of each sandwich.

4 Set a large cast-iron skillet over medium-high heat. Working with one sandwich at a time, place the sandwich mayo-side down in the hot skillet. Spread 1 teaspoon more mayo over the top. Add ½ tablespoon of butter to the pan next to the sandwich and let melt, then tilt the pan to swirl the melted butter around the sandwich. Cook until the cheese has melted and the bread is deeply golden brown, about 2 minutes on each side. Transfer the grilled cheese to a baking sheet and keep warm in the oven while you make the rest.

5 Ladle the soup into bowls and serve with the grilled cheese alongside.

Stracciatella

Serves 4

Stracciata roughly translates from Italian to "mixed up." Dropping eggs into hot broth and whizzing them around in quick circles with a fork as they cook certainly yields a result that is "all mixed up." Mom used to make this for me when I was a kid—it was one of my favorite soups, and to this day, I still find its simple, satisfying flavors a source of comfort. Be sure to season this one to taste: Get the salt just right, and it will be *perfetto*.

4 cups Golden Rotisserie Liquid (page 39) or low-sodium chicken broth
3 large eggs, beaten
5 ounces baby spinach
1 cup freshly grated Parmigiano Reggiano cheese

1 Pour the broth into a large saucepot and bring to a boil over high heat.

2 Using a ladle, stir the broth in a circular motion to create a vortex. While stirring, pour the egg into the outer edge of the vortex so that it gets pulled away, then immediately add the spinach. Use the ladle to push the leaves below the broth.

3 After about 1 minute, turn off the heat; the spinach should be bright green and the eggs should be fully cooked in little strands of yellowish white. Add ½ cup of the cheese and stir to melt.

4 Ladle the soup into bowls, sprinkle evenly with the remaining ½ cup cheese, and serve immediately.

1 CUP

Carrot Ginger Soup

WITH GARLIC CROUTONS

Serves 4

This soup features the classic combination of carrot and ginger, and its beautiful color is a result of simple cooking execution. I've included ground cardamom seeds; they add a numbing spice, not dissimilar to Sichuan peppercorns, that I think goes well with the ginger. It will have people saying, "What is that? It's delicious." The garlic croutons bring a textural contrast and a pop of flavor—an addition that definitely shouldn't be overlooked.

- 2 tablespoons extra-virgin olive oil
- 1 red onion, diced
- 5 garlic cloves, chopped
- 1 (2-inch) piece fresh ginger, peeled and grated
- 1½ teaspoons curry powder
- 1 teaspoon mustard seed
- ⅛ teaspoon black cardamom seeds, ground
- 1 teaspoon kosher salt
- 5 carrots, thinly sliced
- 2 cups low-sodium vegetable broth
- 1 cup crème fraîche
- ¼ cup carrot tops or fresh cilantro, minced
- Garlic Croutons (recipe follows), for serving

1 In a large Dutch oven, heat the olive oil over medium heat. When the oil is shimmering, add the onion, garlic, ginger, curry powder, mustard seed, cardamom seeds, and ½ teaspoon of the salt. Cook, stirring occasionally, until the garlic is golden and the spices are fragrant, about 5 minutes. If the spices begin to burn, add up to 2 tablespoons water and reduce the heat as needed.

2 Add the carrots and the remaining ½ teaspoon salt. Cook over medium heat, stirring occasionally, until the carrots are soft, sweet, and just beginning to show signs of caramelization, about 10 minutes.

3 Pour in the broth and 2 cups water. Increase the heat to high and bring to a boil, then reduce the heat to medium-low and simmer until the carrots are cooked through, 10 to 15 minutes. Remove from the heat. Using an immersion blender, blend the soup directly in the pot until smooth. (Alternatively, carefully transfer the soup to a high-powered blender and blend on medium-low speed until smooth.)

4 In a small bowl, stir together the crème fraîche and carrot tops.

5 Ladle the soup into bowls. Dollop the crème fraîche on top and garnish with garlic croutons before serving.

GARLIC CROUTONS

Makes 3 cups

1 (8- to 10-inch) loaf of sourdough bread, cut into ¼-inch cubes
1½ tablespoons extra-virgin olive oil
1 garlic clove, grated
⅛ teaspoon kosher salt
⅛ teaspoon freshly ground black pepper

Preheat the oven to 350°F. Line a baking sheet with parchment paper. On the prepared baking sheet, combine the bread, olive oil, garlic, salt, and pepper. Toss to coat evenly. Bake for 10 minutes, then use tongs or a spatula to flip the croutons and bake for 7 to 12 minutes more, until golden, toasty, and crunchy all over. Let cool slightly before using or storing. Store in an airtight container at room temperature for up to 10 days.

Golden Rotisserie Liquid

Makes 8 cups

Nothing beats homemade broth, but when you're putting in the time and effort, you might as well make a large batch, and that means you need a lot of bones. With this recipe, you can get all that flavor in about a third of the time, and without having to "save up" a chicken bone graveyard in your kitchen. Here we supplement a fully cooked chicken carcass of any size with a little bouillon paste and use small-cut vegetables (everything should be about ½ inch thick), which allows flavor to be extracted faster. With very little effort, you can fill your kitchen with fantastic aromas and make use of something that would otherwise be thrown away, saving you money. Plus, anything you use this golden liquid in will be that much tastier.

- 1 cooked chicken carcass
- 2 medium onions, sliced
- 2 large carrots, sliced
- 3 celery stalks, sliced
- 1 garlic head, halved crosswise
- 1 bay leaf
- 1 tablespoon coriander seeds
- 1 tablespoon whole black peppercorns
- 2 teaspoons bouillon paste, such as Better Than Bouillon

1 In a large stockpot, combine the carcass, onions, carrots, celery, garlic, bay leaf, coriander, peppercorns, and bouillon. Add enough cool water to fill the pot to 2 inches from the top and bring to an aggressive simmer over medium-high heat. Reduce the heat to low to maintain a gentle simmer. Cook, undisturbed, adjusting the heat as needed and skimming off any dark scum that floats to the top (white foam is okay), until the broth is golden and the vegetables are very soft, about 45 minutes. Remove from the heat.

2 Set a fine-mesh sieve over a large heatproof bowl. Use a spider or slotted spoon to remove and discard the large pieces of bone and vegetables from the broth, then slowly strain the liquid into the bowl. Let cool.

3 Store in airtight containers in the refrigerator for up to 1 week or in the freezer for up to 3 months.

Italian Cobb Salad

WITH CREAMY GORGONZOLA DRESSING

Serves 4

At the height of my obsession with all things Italian in college, I became a bit of a food snob: Shame on Americans who cook sliced prosciutto—Italians wouldn't dare! I've now flipped on that stance, because baked sliced prosciutto is umami-rich, salty, and texturally so crispy, it shatters. That makes it a beautiful addition to salad. This Italian Cobb is a tasty new spin on an old American classic. Even if the old me wouldn't agree, current me says this is the best way to enjoy a Cobb.

For the Dressing

1 heaping cup crumbled Gorgonzola cheese
½ cup mayonnaise
¼ cup plain full-fat yogurt
1 garlic clove, grated
2 tablespoons fresh lemon juice
¼ teaspoon kosher salt, plus more as needed
¼ teaspoon freshly ground black pepper, plus more as needed

For the Salad

2 large eggs
1 head romaine lettuce, chopped
¼ head radicchio, chopped
1 avocado, diced
1 cup cherry tomatoes, halved
2 celery stalks, sliced
1 cup marinated artichoke hearts
6 to 8 pieces Crispy Prosciutto (page 231)

1 MAKE THE DRESSING: In a small bowl, whisk together the Gorgonzola, mayonnaise, yogurt, garlic, lemon juice, salt, and pepper until smooth and well combined. Taste and adjust the seasoning as needed.

2 MAKE THE SALAD: Fill a small pot with 5 inches of water. Bring to a boil over high heat, then, using a spider or slotted spoon, carefully lower the eggs into the water. Cook for 7 minutes. While the eggs are cooking, fill a medium bowl with equal parts water and ice and set it nearby. Transfer the cooked eggs to the ice bath. When they're cool enough to handle, peel the eggs and cut them into quarters.

3 Place the romaine in the bottom of a large serving bowl. Scatter the radicchio over the top. Creating discreet rows, add the avocado, tomatoes, celery, artichokes, prosciutto, and eggs. Top with a generous drizzle of dressing and serve immediately.

Seared Caesar

Serves 4

Classic Caesar dressing uses raw egg yolks, which freaks out a lot of people. So here I've swapped them for mayonnaise, which is an emulsion of egg yolks and oil. The dressing holds together better, is easier to make, and is a little bit heartier—which makes it a perfect pairing for seared lettuce. The real secret is using high-quality oil-packed anchovies, though. This recipe calls for the broiler, but please, if you have an outdoor grill, use it! That's an even better way to get a little smoke (and some fancy grill marks) on your greens.

For the Dressing

6 tablespoons mayonnaise
5 oil-packed anchovy fillets, finely chopped
4 garlic cloves, minced
3 tablespoons freshly grated Parmigiano Reggiano cheese
2 tablespoons fresh lemon juice
1 teaspoon Worcestershire sauce
¼ teaspoon kosher salt, plus more as needed
¼ teaspoon freshly ground black pepper, plus more as needed

For the Salad

2 romaine heads, halved lengthwise through the core
1½ tablespoons extra-virgin olive oil
¼ cup freshly grated Parmigiano Reggiano cheese
¼ cup Pan-Fried Breadcrumbs (page 231) or store-bought seasoned breadcrumbs

1 MAKE THE DRESSING: In a small bowl, whisk together the mayonnaise, anchovies, garlic, cheese, lemon juice, Worcestershire, salt, and pepper. Taste and adjust the seasoning as needed.

2 MAKE THE SALAD: Position an oven rack 6 to 8 inches from the broiler heat source and preheat the broiler. Set a wire rack over a baking sheet.

3 Place the romaine on the rack, cut-side up. Brush the surface of each wedge with olive oil. Sprinkle the romaine wedges with the cheese, dividing it evenly.

4 Broil the romaine for 2 to 5 minutes, until the edges begin to char. Remove from the oven and let cool for 5 to 10 minutes.

5 Arrange the charred romaine wedges on a serving platter and drizzle the dressing over the top, then sprinkle with the breadcrumbs. Serve immediately.

Winter Beets

WITH TARRAGON DRESSING

Serves 4 to 6

I love beets: the color, the taste, the fact that they're not overused. They're a real treat, sweet and earthy, and when roasted, they exhibit a paradoxically soft yet firm resistance upon chewing. This recipe, which is a great addition to any meal, is an exercise in balance between the beets and the cool, bright, creamy dressing. You can roast the beets days in advance and store them in a lidded container in the fridge, then toss them with the dressing just before serving.

For the Beets

- 2 pounds beets (4 to 6 medium), scrubbed
- 2 tablespoons extra-virgin olive oil
- ½ teaspoon kosher salt
- ¼ teaspoon freshly ground black pepper

For the Dressing

- ¼ cup full-fat sour cream
- 2 tablespoons chopped fresh tarragon
- 1 tablespoon Dijon mustard
- ½ teaspoon lemon zest
- 2 tablespoons fresh lemon juice
- ¼ teaspoon freshly ground black pepper
- ⅛ teaspoon kosher salt

1 **MAKE THE BEETS:** Preheat the oven to 400°F.

2 Drizzle the beets with the olive oil and season with salt and pepper. Wrap all of them together in a large sheet of aluminum foil and place them on a baking sheet. Roast for 45 to 90 minutes, depending on the size of the beets, until they are easily pierced with a knife; begin checking for doneness at 45 minutes and in 15-minute increments after that. Remove the beets from the oven, unwrap them, and let cool.

When the beets are cool enough to handle, use a paper towel to rub off their skins. Cut the roasted beets into wedges and place them in a medium bowl.

3 **MEANWHILE, MAKE THE DRESSING:** In a small bowl, whisk together the sour cream, tarragon, Dijon, lemon zest, lemon juice, pepper, and salt.

4 Pour the dressing over the beets and toss to coat. Serve immediately.

STAINLESS STEEL

PASTA

Spicy Rigatoni

WITH FENNEL SAUSAGE RAGÙ

Serves 4 to 6

Bologna, Italy, is where some of the country's greatest culinary creations were born. Among them is *the* ragù, known to the rest of the world as Bolognese. In English, we have wrongly been calling *all* meat sauces Bolognese. The real thing braises for hours, is paired with super-thin egg-based tagliatelle, and is wonderfully elegant. My version takes inspiration from this masterpiece, but it's ready in just thirty minutes. As a result of the faster cooking time, this sauce is a little bit chunky, which makes it a perfect pairing for a hearty boxed pasta. I recommend mezze rigatoni or rigatoni, but any larger, non-twirly pasta will work well and be balanced with this chunky, rustic sauce.

Kosher salt
1 pound dried mezze rigatoni or rigatoni
1 tablespoon extra-virgin olive oil, plus more as needed
1 pound sweet Italian sausage, casings removed
1 teaspoon crushed fennel seeds
2 yellow onions, diced
1 carrot, grated on the large holes of a box grater
1 tablespoon tomato paste
1 teaspoon red pepper flakes
3 tablespoons vodka
1 (14.5-ounce) can crushed tomatoes
¾ cup freshly grated Parmigiano Reggiano cheese, plus more for serving
1 cup packed fresh basil leaves

1 Bring a large pot of salted water to a boil over high heat. Stir in the pasta and cook until al dente according to the package instructions, then reserve 1 cup of the pasta cooking water and drain.

2 Meanwhile, in a large skillet, heat the olive oil over medium heat. When the oil is shimmering, add the sausage and fennel and cook, undisturbed, until the sausage is lightly browned, about 3 minutes, then cook, using a wooden spoon to break up the meat, until no longer pink and lightly caramelized, 2 to 4 minutes.

3 Add the onions and ½ teaspoon salt and cook, stirring occasionally, until the onions just turn golden, about 10 minutes. If the pan seems dry, add another tablespoon of olive oil after about 5 minutes. Add the carrots, tomato paste, and red pepper flakes. Cook, stirring, until the tomato paste is darkened and incorporated, about 1 minute.

4 Pour in the vodka and scrape up any browned bits from the bottom of the pan. Add the tomatoes and 1 cup of water. Bring to a gentle simmer and cook until the sauce thickens and a spoon pulled through leaves a trail, 7 to 10 minutes.

5 Add the cooked pasta to the sauce. Increase the heat to high and cook, stirring, until incorporated, about 1 minute. Remove from the heat, add the cheese and basil, and stir to mix well. If the married sauce and pasta looks a little dry or pasty, stir in ¼ cup of the reserved pasta cooking water at a time and using up to the full 1 cup if needed.

6 Serve immediately, with additional cheese, if desired.

Eggplant Fregola

Serves 4

While many love a falafel sandwich, I've always been more drawn to the sabich sandwich. Fresh pita, deep-fried eggplant, tahini, and Israeli salad, among other fillings, make for a sublime combination. Sandwiches are great for one person, but pasta serves a crowd! Fregola is my pasta of choice because it cooks quickly in minimal water and holds its texture well thanks to its tiny pearl shape. If you can't find fregola, pearl (Israeli) couscous will do. Be sure to cut the eggplant, onion, and cucumber into similar-size pieces (about ¼ inch) so every bite is perfect. If you haven't yet had a sabich sandwich, try one after you've made this dish—you'll taste where the inspiration came from.

Kosher salt
1 heaping cup dried fregola
1 eggplant, cubed
3 tablespoons neutral oil
1 tablespoon extra-virgin olive oil
1 small red onion, diced
½ cup dried cranberries
1 tablespoon balsamic vinegar
1 heaping cup halved cherry tomatoes
1 cup cubed cucumber
Zest and juice of 1 large lemon
1 cup fresh Italian parsley, chopped
1 tablespoon tahini
½ teaspoon honey
⅛ teaspoon flaky salt

1 Bring a large pot of salted water to a boil over high heat. Add the fregola and cook until al dente according to the package instructions. Drain the fregola in a fine-mesh sieve and rinse with cold water until cool to the touch.

2 Meanwhile, heat a large skillet over medium-high heat for about 1 minute. Add half of the eggplant and 1 teaspoon salt. Cook, stirring vigorously, until the eggplant begins to release moisture, about 2 minutes. Add 1½ tablespoons of the neutral oil. Cook, shaking the pan occasionally, until the eggplant is browned, about 8 minutes. Transfer the eggplant to a plate. Repeat with the remaining eggplant, another 1 teaspoon salt, and the remaining 1½ tablespoons neutral oil. Transfer the remaining eggplant to the plate.

3 In the same skillet, heat the olive oil over medium heat. When the oil is shimmering, add the onion and ¼ teaspoon salt. Cook, stirring, until golden, 5 to 7 minutes. Add the dried cranberries and vinegar. Cook, scraping up any browned bits from the bottom of the pan, about 1 minute. Remove from the heat.

4 In a medium bowl, combine the fregola with the eggplant, onion, cranberries, cherry tomatoes, cucumber, lemon zest, lemon juice, parsley, tahini, and honey. Toss to combine, then finish with flaky salt. Serve at room temperature.

Pasta with Mozzarella

Serves 4 to 6

When I tell you I craved this pasta every day of my life from age four all the way to age fifteen, I'm not kidding. My mom would cut up the pieces of mozzarella and tuck them into her version of Marcella Hazan's classic tomato sauce. The chew, the salt, the cheese pull, the fact that I had to hunt for hidden treasures—all of it made me excited for bite after bite. Cherry tomatoes give this an inherent freshness that *feels like summertime*, regardless of the current season. When pierced, they bleed their juices to make a sauce, sorcery assisted by white wine and the covering of the pan. I eventually learned that Italian restaurants would make this for me if I asked, even if it wasn't on the menu—until 2001, when I was flatly told no at Lupa (the restaurant I'd later work at). They nudged me in the direction of a different dish that was another kind of revelation, but I'll share that story with you some other time.

Kosher salt
1 pound dried calamarata, paccheri, or rigatoni
3 tablespoons extra-virgin olive oil
4 garlic cloves, sliced
1 tablespoon tomato paste
3 tablespoons dry white wine
2 pints cherry tomatoes, each pierced with a fork, or 1 (28-ounce) can crushed tomatoes
1 cup loosely packed fresh basil leaves
8 ounces chilled fresh mozzarella (see page 21), cut into ¼-inch cubes

1 Bring a large pot of salted water to a boil over high heat. Add the pasta and cook until 1 minute shy of al dente according to the package instructions, then drain.

2 Meanwhile, place a large skillet over medium heat. Pour in the olive oil and add the garlic and cook until the garlic is sizzling and lightly golden on its edges, 3 to 5 minutes. Add the tomato paste and cook, stirring, until the paste darkens, about 1 minute. Pour in the wine and cook until the alcohol evaporates, about 1 minute. (It will sputter; cover the pan until it quiets down.)

3 Increase the heat to high, add the cherry tomatoes, and season with ½ teaspoon salt. Add ½ cup of the basil and stir to wilt and combine, about 1 minute.

4 Use a spider or tongs to transfer the pasta to the sauce. Increase the heat to high and cook, stirring, until the pasta is cooked through but still al dente, about 2 minutes. Remove from the heat. Add the mozzarella and the remaining ½ cup basil. Stir until well combined, divide among plates, and serve immediately.

Steamed Onion Stroganoff

Serves 4

We've had so many decades to evolve and perfect recipes, and we know the science behind what makes things taste great. Caramelized onions are universally accepted as "the best-tasting onions," so it's easy to follow the status quo. In traditional stroganoff, that means cooking a lot of elements separately so that each is the best they can be. But in my opinion, that's too fussy for such a humble dish. (Kind of like the time I made it with an entire bottle of $100 wine. I was a teenager, I didn't know! But it sure was good.) Let's make it extra easy: In this version, the beef cooks first, then the mushrooms go in to absorb the drippings, and finally the onions are steamed. The whole thing is juicy and delicious and leans a lot more toward hamburger—a perfect one-pot meal perfect for any night of the week.

Kosher salt
12 ounces dried egg noodles
3 tablespoons unsalted butter
1 pound 85% lean ground beef
2 teaspoons sweet paprika
1 pound cremini mushrooms, thinly sliced
1 small yellow onion, chopped
2 garlic cloves, chopped
½ teaspoon dried thyme
1 tablespoon all-purpose flour
1½ cups low-sodium beef broth or vegetable broth
1 tablespoon Worcestershire sauce
½ teaspoon Dijon mustard
⅓ cup full-fat sour cream
Flaky salt
Chopped fresh parsley, for serving (optional)

1 Bring a large pot of salted water to a boil over high heat. Add the egg noodles and cook until al dente according to the package instructions. Drain the noodles.

2 Meanwhile, in a large skillet, melt the butter over medium-high heat. Add the beef, 1 teaspoon salt, and the paprika and cook, breaking up the beef with a wooden spoon, until it's cooked through and no longer pink, 6 to 8 minutes. Add the mushrooms and cook, stirring to coat, until they plump up and look juicy, about 5 minutes.

3 Stir in the onion, garlic, and thyme. Reduce the heat to low, cover, and cook until the onion is soft and translucent, 10 minutes.

4 Remove the lid, increase the heat to medium, and stir in the flour until completely incorporated, about 1 minute. Pour in the broth, Worcestershire, and Dijon. Increase the heat to medium-high and bring the sauce to a simmer. Cook, stirring frequently, until the sauce thickens, 5 to 7 minutes.

5 Remove from the heat and stir in the sour cream to combine. Divide the noodles among bowls, then spoon the sauce over the top. Finish with flaky salt and parsley, if desired, before serving.

Cold Peanut Noodles

Serves 4

I haven't yet been to China and I've always known that the Chinese food I grew up eating was very Americanized (though still delicious). So when Han Dynasty opened its first location in downtown New York, the buzz they had created in Philadelphia with "Chinese food from China" moved north. "This is the first *real* Sichuan restaurant America!" people were exclaiming. Could a dining experience transport me without my physically traveling? Their dan dan noodles—sesame-coated noodles with minced pork and lots of hot peppers—are still a hot-ticket item. At first bite, it was *really* spicy, and I loved it. Before long, I tolerated the spice and started picking out individual flavors. My recipe uses my favorite elements of Chinese five-spice powder (a blend that can, in fact, have *more* than five spices), and is nostalgic to the takeout I grew up with.

- 8 ounces dried lo mein noodles
- ½ cup creamy peanut butter
- 1½ tablespoons sugar
- 1 tablespoon low-sodium soy sauce
- 2 teaspoons fresh lime juice
- 1 tablespoon distilled white vinegar
- 2 tablespoons neutral oil
- 1 tablespoon chopped garlic
- 1½ teaspoons grated fresh ginger
- ¼ teaspoon ground fennel seeds
- ¼ teaspoon red pepper flakes

For Serving

- ¼ cup sliced scallions
- 2 tablespoons sesame seeds
- Chili crisp
- Sweet & Zingy Fresno Chilies (page 230) or store-bought sliced banana peppers (optional)

1 Bring a large pot of water to a boil over high heat. Add the noodles and cook according to the package instructions. Drain the noodles and rinse with cool water.

2 Meanwhile, in a large bowl, stir together the peanut butter, sugar, soy sauce, lime juice, and vinegar.

3 In a small saucepan, combine the neutral oil, garlic, ginger, fennel, and red pepper flakes. Cook over medium-high heat, stirring often, until the ginger is deeply golden and the smaller pieces of garlic are just beginning to char, 4 to 6 minutes.

4 Using a rubber spatula, transfer the garlic-ginger mixture to the bowl with the peanut butter. Mix well to combine. Add the noodles and continue mixing. The sauce should be smooth and creamy, not clumpy; add up to 2 tablespoons of water to loosen it, if needed.

5 Divide among bowls, top with scallions, the sesame seeds, and chili crisp (or your favorite toppings!), and serve.

Beet Risotto

Serves 4

This risotto is inspired by one of my all-time favorite pasta dishes (which hasn't quite reached the US yet): casunziei all'Ampezzana, which I've been lucky to enjoy many times in the northern Italian town Cortina d'Ampezzo. *Casunziei* translates to "little pockets" in the local dialect, Ampezzano. Four-inch circles of thin fresh pasta are filled with cooked pureed beets then folded over to make perfect half-moons, which are served in a sauce of poppy seeds and Parmigiano cheese. It's a totally unexpected, simple, and delicious dish. I've turned it into a risotto because it's a lot easier to make; the color on the plate is even more pronounced, and it's still unexpected, sweet, and smile-inducing. Pro tip: Preheat your bowls in the oven on the lowest setting possible before serving, which will slow the clumping of the risotto tableside. Oh, and eat it with a spoon.

- 6 cups low-sodium vegetable broth
- 2 to 3 red beets, cut into ¼-inch dice or grated on the large holes of a box grater, ends reserved
- 1 tablespoon extra-virgin olive oil
- 1 cup Arborio rice
- 1 small yellow onion, diced
- ½ cup dry white wine
- 3 ounces crème fraîche or goat cheese
- ½ cup freshly grated Parmigiano Reggiano cheese
- Kosher salt
- 3 tablespoons unsalted butter
- 1 tablespoon poppy seeds
- 10 fresh sage leaves

1 In a medium pot, bring the broth to a simmer over medium heat. Add the beet ends for more color.

2 Meanwhile, in a large saucepan, combine the beets, olive oil, rice, and onion over medium heat. Cook, stirring, until the rice is toasted, about 2 minutes. Pour in the wine and cook until the alcohol evaporates, about 1 minute. Add just enough of the hot broth to cover the rice, about ¾ cup or 1 ladleful. Cook, stirring, until the rice has absorbed the liquid, about 3 minutes. Continue adding broth, stirring continuously and allowing the liquid to be completely absorbed between additions. After 5 additions of broth, taste the rice for doneness: It should be firm but cooked. If not, add another bit of broth (or water, if you've run out of broth). When the rice is done, remove it from the heat.

3 Add the crème fraîche and cheese and stir to incorporate. Taste and add salt in ½-teaspoon increments as needed.

4 Meanwhile, melt the butter in a small skillet over medium-high heat. When the butter begins to brown, swirl the pan and add the poppy seeds and sage. Cook until the popping stops, 1 to 2 minutes.

5 Divide the risotto among warmed bowls and pour the brown butter sauce over the top. Enjoy immediately.

STAINLESS STEEL

Super Garlic Spaghetti

Serves 4

In Italian American households, spaghetti aglio e olio is equivalent to a packet of ramen noodles. There's no dish I've eaten more than this one—but my plate always had a pool of oil sitting at the bottom, and I needed to restir the dish as I ate it. By slowly cooking the garlic cloves while they're fully submerged in oil (a technique called confiting), the cloves become so soft that when mixed with the spaghetti, they emulsify with the oil to create a sauce. The sauce sticks better to the pasta and completely changes the texture. (Don't be mad at me for making it better, Italy!) You'll want all your garlic cloves to be about the same size, so cut any big ones as needed before confiting them.

½ cup extra-virgin olive oil
1 heaping cup peeled garlic cloves (about 12)
1 bay leaf
1 teaspoon red pepper flakes
2 tablespoons kosher salt
1 pound dried spaghetti
½ cup freshly grated Parmigiano Reggiano cheese
1 medium bunch parsley, finely chopped
Flaky salt

1 In a small skillet, combine the olive oil, garlic, and bay leaf. Bring to a gentle simmer over medium-low heat, reducing the heat as needed if the simmering becomes too aggressive. Cook until the garlic is golden and so soft it collapses under the slightest pressure from a fork, about 30 minutes. Remove from the heat, discard the bay leaf, and stir in the red pepper flakes. Set aside 4 tablespoons of the garlic oil (reserve the rest for another use) and all the confited garlic cloves.

2 Meanwhile, bring a large pot of water to a boil over high heat. Add the salt and the spaghetti. Cook until just shy of al dente, a few minutes less than the package instructions. Reserve 2 cups of the pasta cooking water, then drain the pasta and return it to the hot pot.

3 Add the confited garlic and 3 tablespoons of the garlic oil to the pasta. Cook over high heat, stirring continuously, until the garlic cloves melt away, about 1 minute. Add the cheese, parsley, and ½ cup of the reserved pasta cooking water and stir to combine. Add another ¾ cup of the reserved water and stir until smooth.

4 Divide the pasta among plates. Drizzle with the remaining 1 tablespoon garlic oil, if desired, dividing it evenly, and sprinkle with flaky salt. Serve immediately.

Summer Pasta

Serves 4

I've always loved the *idea* of pasta primavera, but never loved the dish itself. Something about the versions that I grew up with remind me of school cafeteria food (maybe it's those always subpar carrots), so how could I change it? My concept fast-forwards the harvest season and really leans into the American summer vibe. Corn and onions sautéed together in olive oil is the combination at the heart of this dish—and it tastes great hot or at room temperature.

Kosher salt
1 pound dried fusilli
3 tablespoons extra-virgin olive oil
1 large red onion, thinly sliced
2 cups fresh or frozen corn
1 large zucchini, diced
1 cup coarsely chopped sun-dried tomatoes
1 tablespoon finely chopped fresh chives
¼ cup fresh mint leaves, torn, for serving
¼ cup Pan-Fried Breadcrumbs (page 231) or store-bought seasoned breadcrumbs, for serving
Red pepper flakes, for serving

1 Bring a large pot of salted water to a boil over high heat. Add the fusilli and cook until al dente according to the package instructions. Reserve ½ cup of the pasta cooking water and drain the pasta.

2 Meanwhile, in a large saucepan, heat 2 tablespoons of the olive oil over medium-high heat. When the oil is shimmering, add the onion and 1 teaspoon salt. Cook, stirring occasionally, until the onions have reduced in volume by half and are just beginning to brown, about 10 minutes. Add the corn and zucchini and cook, stirring occasionally, until the zucchini begins to soften, about 5 minutes.

3 Add the sun-dried tomatoes and ¼ cup of the reserved pasta cooking water. Reduce the heat to medium, stir well, and cook until the onions are jammy and the zucchini is soft, about 10 minutes. There should be no excess liquid in the pan, but it shouldn't be dry.

4 Add the pasta to the sauce, increase the heat to high, and cook, stirring, until well combined, about 1 minute. Add more pasta cooking water if it looks dry. Remove from the heat. Stir in the chives and the remaining 1 tablespoon olive oil.

5 Divide the pasta among plates. Finish each plate with the mint, breadcrumbs, and red pepper flakes before serving.

Super Cheesy Shells

Serves 4 to 6

In 2007, I entered a mac-and-cheese-making contest in Brooklyn. I had no idea what I was doing back then and my concept was to focus on colors: yellow cheese and black (sepia) pasta. It was only good for five minutes, and then the cheese seized up. I now know the secret to a really good mac is to start with a combination of flour and fat (called a roux) and add milk to that (transforming it into a béchamel). When the cheese is added to the béchamel—it will flow like lava. *This* is the homemade mac and cheese of my dreams, and the one I wish I'd entered into that contest. It's loaded with sweet garlic, three cheeses, and spinach to add even more flavor. You can freeze any leftovers in an oven-safe baking dish for up to 3 months; reheat in a 400°F oven, covered with foil, for 40 minutes, then uncover and heat for 20 minutes more.

Kosher salt
1 pound dried pasta shells
½ cup (1 stick) unsalted butter
10 garlic cloves, smashed and peeled
½ teaspoon freshly ground black pepper
3 tablespoons all-purpose flour
1¾ cups whole milk
8 ounces Muenster cheese, cubed or torn
8 ounces fresh mozzarella cheese, cubed
2 cups freshly grated Parmigiano Reggiano cheese
10 ounces baby spinach

1 Position an oven rack 8 inches from the broiler heat source and preheat the broiler.

2 Bring a large pot of salted water to a boil over high heat. Add the pasta shells and cook until al dente according to the package instructions. Drain the pasta.

3 Meanwhile, in a medium pot, melt the butter over medium heat. Add the garlic, 1 teaspoon salt, and the pepper. Cook, swirling the pan to submerge the garlic, until the garlic is lightly golden and beginning to brown at the edges, about 5 minutes. Whisk in the flour until it is incorporated and the mixture thickens, about 2 minutes.

4 Whisking continuously, add half the milk. Bring the sauce to a gentle simmer and add the remaining milk, still whisking. Add the Muenster, mozzarella, and 1 cup of the Parmigiano. Whisk until smooth. Return the sauce to a low simmer and add half of the spinach, stirring to wilt, about 1 minute. Repeat with the remaining spinach and continue to fold and stir until it has fully wilted into the sauce, another minute or so.

5 Gently fold the cooked shells into the sauce. Taste and adjust the salt as needed. Transfer the pasta mixture to a 9 × 13-inch baking dish and smooth out the top. Top with the remaining 1 cup Parmigiano.

6 Broil for about 5 minutes, or until the top is golden brown, keeping a close eye on it. Remove from the oven and let cool for 5 minutes. Divide among bowls and serve.

BREAD & PIZZA

Avocado Toast Twins

Each serves 2

If my dad and I wake up in the same house, we'll most likely start the morning with a bike ride or hitting tennis balls for a few hours, so he always makes us his signature breakfast at five a.m.: a single piece of toast with butter, jam, and a poached egg, the cooking of which he nails every time. Adding avocado makes it more substantial and allows larger slices of bread to be used without the fear of too few toppings. It's a perfect start to an active day. Later on when I'm running on empty, I want carbohydrates, salt, and general heft, so this second toast hits those marks for me. Chunks of avocado, sun-dried tomato, and olive offer a meaty and savory bite that could be a brunch, lunch, or snack.

THE BREKKIE

3 teaspoons strawberry preserves
2 slices sourdough bread, toasted
1 avocado, halved
2 large eggs
1½ teaspoons distilled white vinegar
½ teaspoon freshly ground black pepper
¼ teaspoon flaky salt

1 Fill a medium saucepan with water and bring to a boil over high heat.

2 Meanwhile, spread 1½ teaspoons of the strawberry preserves on each slice of toast. Scoop or squeeze an avocado half onto each slice, then use a fork to mash and spread the avocado edge to edge.

3 Crack each egg into a small bowl or ramekin. When the water is boiling, reduce the heat to maintain a gentle simmer, add the vinegar, then use a large slotted spoon to swirl the water clockwise to create a vortex. Drop each egg into the center of the vortex. Cook for 3 minutes, then use a slotted spoon to remove the eggs one at a time. Gently lay them on a clean kitchen towel to drain for about 1 minute.

4 Top each toast slice with a poached egg, then season with the pepper and flaky salt. Cut the egg in half so the yolk runs and enjoy at once.

THE SLEEPER

2 slices sourdough bread, toasted
1 avocado, diced
8 pitted green olives, halved
4 sun-dried tomatoes, quartered
1½ teaspoons extra-virgin olive oil
⅛ teaspoon flaky salt
⅛ teaspoon freshly ground black pepper

1 Scatter the avocado cubes onto the toast slices, dividing them evenly, then intersperse the sun-dried tomatoes and olives among the avocado.

2 Drizzle each toast with the olive oil and finish with the flaky salt and pepper.

Meatball Sub

Serves 4

My relationship with the New York deli started with bagels and meatball sandwiches. Before the school bus picked me up, I'd steal the quarters my mom kept for parking meters. The deli was right by my stop. For 75 cents I could have a TBB—a toasted buttered bagel. If I had $1.25, I could get the TBB with B—bacon. (Yes, we nine-year-old boys ordered this way.) One morning, I didn't realize I was short, but the cashier knew me and said, "Pay us later." I came back after school a few days later with the change I owed—and that's when I saw the lunch spread for the first time and my love for the meatball sub began. It needs to be saucy, hot, and in my hands fast. There's no searing of the meatballs here; skipping it saves time and doesn't take away from the vibe.

For the Sauce

1 (28-ounce) can crushed tomatoes
1 large basil sprig

For the Meatballs

¼ cup Italian seasoned breadcrumbs
¼ cup whole milk
1 large egg
3 garlic cloves, grated
½ small yellow onion, grated
2 tablespoons freshly grated Parmigiano Reggiano or Pecorino Romano cheese
2 tablespoons chopped fresh Italian parsley
1 teaspoon kosher salt
½ teaspoon freshly ground black pepper
¼ teaspoon red pepper flakes
½ pound ground pork
½ pound 85% lean ground beef

For the Sandwich

2 (12-inch) Italian semolina or ciabatta loaves, halved lengthwise
5 ounces provolone cheese, sliced
½ cup Sweet & Zingy Fresno Chilies (page 230) or store-bought sliced pickled banana peppers

1 MAKE THE SAUCE: In a large, deep saucepan, combine the crushed tomatoes and the basil. Cover and cook over medium heat, stirring occasionally, until the sauce has reduced slightly and the flavors have melded, about 20 minutes.

2 MEANWHILE, MAKE THE MEATBALLS: In a large bowl, combine the breadcrumbs, milk, and egg and stir well to combine. Let stand until the breadcrumbs have absorbed the liquid, about 3 minutes. Add the garlic, onion, Parmigiano, parsley, salt, black pepper, and red pepper flakes. Whisk to combine well. Add the pork and beef and, using your hands, gently mix to incorporate. Divide the meat mixture into 12 equal portions and roll them between your palms into balls slightly larger than a golf ball.

3 Gently place the meatballs in the simmering sauce. Cover and cook, flipping halfway through, until the meatballs are firm to the touch and the sauce has reduced slightly, 40 minutes. Remove the pot from the heat.

4 MAKE THE SANDWICH: Place an oven rack 6 to 8 inches from the broiler heat source and preheat the broiler. Set a wire rack over a baking sheet.

5 Place the bread on the prepared rack, cut-side up. Spoon several tablespoons of sauce on each piece of bread. Add 6 meatballs to each of the bottom halves. Lay the provolone over the top and bottom pieces of bread, dividing it evenly between both sandwiches. Broil for 1 to 2 minutes, until the cheese is golden brown and bubbling. Remove from the oven.

6 Top the cheesy meatballs with the Fresno peppers. Close up the sandwiches and slice each in half. Serve immediately.

Everything Soft Pretzel Knots

WITH MUSTARD DIPPING SAUCE

Makes 24 pretzel knots

Before I knew how to cook from scratch, the freezer was always my culinary starting point, and frozen pretzels were a staple. Wetting frozen pretzels so the addition of pretzel salt would adhere before baking became a ritual I enjoyed. I now know that one of life's great culinary joys is the aroma of freshly baked bread, which is why I've taken that childhood memory and elevated it. When making pretzels, the dough must be quickly boiled in water with baking soda added to give them their dark color and unique flavor. I use everything bagel seasoning, but feel free to make your own spice/seed blend.

- 2½ cups (300g) all-purpose flour, plus more as needed
- 1 (¼-ounce/7g) packet instant yeast
- 2 tablespoons sugar
- 1 teaspoon kosher salt
- 1 cup (240ml) whole milk
- 2 tablespoons unsalted butter, melted
- Nonstick cooking spray
- ⅓ cup (75g) baking soda
- 1 large egg yolk, beaten
- 3 tablespoons everything bagel seasoning
- ½ cup Honey Mustard Sauce (page 227) or store-bought honey mustard, for serving

1 In the bowl of a stand mixer fitted with the dough hook, combine the flour, yeast, sugar, and salt. Whisk to mix well. Add the milk and melted butter, then mix on low speed until combined, about 1 minute. Increase the speed to medium and knead until the dough is soft and elastic, about 5 minutes. The dough should clear the sides of the bowl, but lightly stick on the bottom. If the dough sticks to the sides after 2 to 3 minutes, add another tablespoon of flour.

2 Coat a large bowl with nonstick spray. Place the dough in the bowl, cover with plastic wrap, and let rest in a warm space until doubled in size, about 1 hour.

3 Preheat the oven to 425°F. Line two baking sheets with parchment paper.

4 Turn out the dough onto a clean work surface. Punch the dough down, then divide it into 24 equal pieces, each about the size of a golf ball. Roll each piece into a 6-inch rope, then tie the rope in a knot, tucking any excess underneath. Place on the prepared baking sheets, spacing them 1 inch apart. Cover with clean kitchen towels and let rest in a warm place for about 20 minutes. The knots should be puffy and spring back slowly when touched.

5 In a large, high-sided pot, combine 6 cups water and the baking soda. Bring to a boil over high heat. Add 3 or 4 pretzel knots and cook, flipping halfway, for about 30 seconds. Using a slotted spoon, return the boiled pretzels to the baking sheet. Repeat with the remaining dough. Brush the tops and sides of each boiled knot with egg yolk and sprinkle generously with everything bagel seasoning.

6 Bake for 10 to 12 minutes, swapping and rotating the baking sheets halfway through, until the pretzels are baked through and deeply golden brown on top. Transfer to a wire rack and let cool to room temperature. Serve with the honey mustard alongside for dipping.

Cuban Reuben

Makes 2 large sandwiches

I'll admit it: The name of this sandwich rhymes, and that's the reason I wanted to make it. As a New York native, I've tasted the best Reubens, but the cold winters have often drawn me down to the warmer Miami air, where I can't help but consume as many Cubanos as possible. I love them both. To make a true Cubano at home, you'd need to roast a lot of pork for many hours . . . but what if you swapped the roasted pork for pastrami? Could you fuse a New York deli staple with a Florida classic? Would it work? The answer is yes, every single time.

For the Sauerkraut Slaw

1 cup sauerkraut, drained
2 kosher dill pickles, finely chopped
¼ small red onion, thinly sliced

For the Sauce

¼ cup spicy brown mustard
2 tablespoons yellow mustard
2 tablespoons mayonnaise

For the Sandwich

2 tablespoons unsalted butter, at room temperature
2 (10-inch) hoagie rolls, halved lengthwise
10 ounces pastrami, thinly sliced
8 ounces boiled deli ham, thinly sliced
8 ounces Swiss cheese, thinly sliced

1 **MAKE THE SLAW:** In a small bowl, combine the sauerkraut, pickles, and onion. Mix with a fork to combine well.

2 **MAKE THE SAUCE:** In a small bowl, whisk together the spicy brown mustard, yellow mustard, and mayonnaise.

3 **MAKE THE SANDWICH:** Lightly butter the outsides of the hoagie rolls, tops and bottoms. Spread the sauce on the insides, tops and bottoms, dividing evenly.

4 Onto the bottom buns, layer the pastrami, ham, Swiss, and slaw, dividing evenly. Add the top buns and gently press to seal.

5 Heat a large skillet over medium-low heat. Place the buttered sandwiches into the skillet, lay a small sheet of aluminum foil or parchment paper over the sandwiches, then add a second, heavy skillet on top to press. Cook until the cheese begins to melt and the bottoms of the sandwiches are golden brown, 3 to 5 minutes. Remove the top skillet, flip the sandwiches, and re-cover with the foil and weight. Cook until the other sides are golden brown, 2 to 4 minutes more.

6 Transfer the sandwiches to a cutting board and let cool for about 1 minute. Slice and serve.

Buttermilk Sage Rolls

WITH WHIPPED MAPLE BUTTER

Makes 15 rolls

Sometimes you need a little road trip to feel inspired in the kitchen. While I've certainly explored that idea with my cooking show *Worth the Hype*, I've started driving pretty far distances from my home for the same reason. Every season, I stop into a place called Community Table in the middle of Litchfield County, Connecticut, about an hour from where I live. Their menu is fantastic, hyperlocal, seasonal, and elegant. Without fail, the first item listed is homemade rolls with whipped butter. I've had their six-grain sourdough rolls with honey butter and cardamom rolls with smoked butter, among others. They've made me realize that soft, hot, fresh bread and butter are a good enough reason to breathe air. This combination incorporates my two favorite winter flavors, sage and maple syrup.

For the Rolls

- 4 tablespoons (½ stick/56g) unsalted butter
- 2 tablespoons chopped fresh sage, or 1 tablespoon dried
- 4⅓ cups (520g) bread flour, plus more for dusting
- ¼ cup (50g) sugar
- 1 tablespoon kosher salt
- 1 (¼-ounce/7g) packet instant yeast
- 1½ cups (350g) buttermilk
- 2 large eggs
- Nonstick cooking spray

For the Whipped Maple Butter

- ½ cup (1 stick) unsalted butter
- ¼ cup pure maple syrup
- ¼ teaspoon kosher salt

1 MAKE THE ROLLS: In a small heatproof bowl, combine the butter and sage. Microwave in 30-second increments until the butter is melted. (Alternatively, combine the butter and sage in a small saucepan and cook over low heat until the butter is fully melted.) Let cool slightly.

2 In the bowl of a stand mixer fitted with the dough hook, combine the bread flour, sugar, salt, and yeast. Whisk to mix well. Add the buttermilk, 1 of the eggs, and the cooled butter mixture. Mix on low speed until most of the flour has been incorporated, about 1 minute. Increase the speed to medium-high and mix until the dough pulls away from the sides and is soft and elastic, about 5 minutes.

3 Coat a large bowl with nonstick spray, then transfer the dough to the bowl. Cover with plastic wrap and let rest in a warm space until doubled in size, 1 to 2 hours.

4 Coat a 9 × 13-inch baking dish with nonstick spray. Dust a clean work surface with flour and turn out the dough onto it. Use a bench scraper or knife to divide the dough into 15 equal-size pieces. Form each dough piece into a round by tucking the outer corners into the middle to form a rough ball shape, then rubbing it between your palms; the balls should be 2 to 3 inches in diameter. If the dough sticks to your hands, dust them with a small amount of flour.

5 Place the dough balls in the prepared baking dish. Cover lightly with plastic wrap and let rest in a warm place again to rise for 30 to 60 minutes. They're ready for baking when you press them gently with your finger and the dough slowly springs back.

6 In a small bowl, beat the remaining 1 egg. Lightly brush the surface of the

Recipe continues

dough balls with the egg. Bake for about 20 minutes, or until the surface of the rolls is deeply golden brown.

7 Transfer the baking dish to a wire rack and let cool for 15 minutes in the pan. Then carefully flip the rolls out and return them to the rack.

8 MEANWHILE, MAKE THE MAPLE BUTTER: In a small saucepan, melt the butter over medium heat. Continue cooking, swirling the pan and stirring frequently, until the butter is deep golden brown, about 3 minutes.

9 Remove from the heat. Add the maple syrup and salt; the mixture will sputter and bubble. When the sputtering stops, whisk to mix well. Return to low heat and cook until the large bubbles dissipate, 1 to 2 minutes.

10 Transfer the saucepan, with the whisk in it, to the refrigerator to cool. Whisk the mixture every 5 minutes, reincorporating the maple syrup into the butter; it will look separated and a bit lumpy. When the butter has cooled to room temperature, after about 20 minutes, remove it from the refrigerator and whisk assertively to fully combine, 30 to 60 seconds.

11 Serve the rolls while still warm with the maple butter.

Honey Mustard Tomato Galette

Serves 8

I love a savory pastry, but cute little individual portions aren't what I'm about. I want a meal! Inspired by puff pastry tomato tartlets that sit behind the glass of French bakeries, I wanted to go bigger. More dough! Honey mustard! This galette is a meal: a buttery, flaky piecrust adorned with a simple honey mustard tomato salad. And if we're calling it a tomato salad, why not make it an actual salad by adding arugula and sliced red onions? Spicy, sweet, juicy, savory, and familiar in so many ways. This galette will awaken food memories you didn't expect.

For the Galette Dough

- 1½ cups plus 3 tablespoons (210g) all-purpose flour, plus more for dusting
- 1 tablespoon sugar
- ½ teaspoon kosher salt
- 10 tablespoons (1¼ sticks/140g) unsalted butter, cubed and chilled
- 7 tablespoons (105ml) ice water, plus more if needed
- 1 large egg yolk, beaten

For the Toppings

- 4 (¼-inch-thick) ring slices of red onion
- 1 tablespoon extra-virgin olive oil
- 1 teaspoon kosher salt
- 8 tomatoes on the vine, cut into ¼-inch-thick slices (see Note, page 80)
- 3 cups arugula
- 1 tablespoon Honey Mustard Sauce (page 227), or store-bought honey mustard

1 MAKE THE DOUGH: In a food processor, combine the flour, sugar, and salt and process to combine, about 10 seconds. Add the butter and pulse in quick, short spurts until you have pea-size pieces, about 15 total pulses. Add 5 tablespoons of the ice water and pulse 5 times to begin combining. Add the remaining 2 tablespoons ice water and pulse until the mixture forms a ball. The dough should not be tacky or wet, but there should be no dry patches of flour. If needed, add more ice water 1 tablespoon at a time.

2 Turn out the dough onto a clean, lightly floured work surface and form it into a 6-inch disc, 2 inches thick. Wrap in plastic wrap and refrigerate for at least 1 hour and up to 2 days.

3 MAKE THE TOPPINGS: In a medium bowl, combine the onion rings, olive oil, and salt. Separate the onion rings from each other, mix well to coat, and set aside.

4 Preheat the oven to 400°F. Line a baking sheet with parchment paper.

5 Lightly flour a clean work surface. Remove the dough from the refrigerator and roll it into a 14-inch round. If it's too stiff to roll out, let it stand for 5 minutes, then try again.

6 Working quickly is the name of the game, we want to keep that dough as cold as possible. Marble countertops are helpful in maintaining that chill. You can always pop the galette back into the fridge to keep it cool and firm.

7 Transfer the dough to the prepared baking sheet; there should be some overhang. If the dough feels too soft to the touch, transfer it to the freezer to firm up slightly, 3 to 5 minutes. Cover the entire surface of the dough with the tomato slices, leaving a 2-inch border of dough. Top the tomatoes with the dressed onions.

Recipe continues

8 Fold the edges of the galette dough into the center, pleating the edges to fully close it in. Brush the crust with the egg yolk. If the crust feels too soft again, place it in the freezer for 3 to 5 minutes more until mostly firm to the touch.

9 Bake the galette for 40 to 50 minutes, until the crust is deeply golden brown. Remove from the oven, then let rest for 5 minutes.

10 In a medium bowl, combine the arugula and the honey mustard sauce and toss well.

11 Top the galette with the arugula, slice, and serve.

NOTE: If the sliced tomatoes look extra juicy, lay them out on paper towels to absorb some of the liquid while you roll out the dough. Otherwise, they might make the dough soggy.

Balsamic Strawberry Galette, page 83

Honey Mustard Tomato Galette

Balsamic Strawberry Galette

Serves 8

A galette has the same delicious buttery crust as a pie because it is a pie—a *free-form* pie. No pie pan needed; irregular dough shapes are encouraged. This strawberry galette started out as a strawberry cream pie and evolved into a balsamic vinegar–infused free-form pie filled with goat cheese. It's sweet, fruity, and buttery. The simplicity of this filling should inspire you to experiment with other galettes!

For the Dough

- 1½ cups plus 3 tablespoons (210g) all-purpose flour, plus more for dusting
- 1 tablespoon sugar
- ½ teaspoon kosher salt
- 10 tablespoons (1¼ sticks/140g) unsalted butter, cubed and chilled
- 7 tablespoons (105ml) ice water, plus more if needed
- 1 large egg yolk, beaten

For the Filling

- 8 ounces goat cheese, at room temperature
- 2 tablespoons pure maple syrup
- ¼ teaspoon kosher salt
- ¼ teaspoon freshly ground black pepper

For the Balsamic Strawberries

- 1 tablespoon cornstarch
- 3 tablespoons balsamic vinegar
- 1 pound fresh strawberries, halved
- ⅓ cup sugar
- ½ teaspoon kosher salt

To Finish

- 1 tablespoon honey, for drizzling
- 1 teaspoon flaky salt

1 MAKE THE DOUGH: In a food processor, combine the flour, sugar, and salt and process to combine, about 10 seconds. Add the butter and pulse in quick, short spurts until you have pea-size pieces, about 15 total pulses. Add 5 tablespoons of the ice water and pulse 5 times to begin combining. Add the remaining 2 tablespoons ice water and pulse until the mixture forms a ball. The dough should not be tacky or wet, but there should be no dry patches of flour. If needed, add more ice water 1 tablespoon at a time.

2 Turn out the dough onto a clean, lightly floured work surface and form it into a 6-inch disc, 2 inches thick. Wrap in plastic wrap and refrigerate for at least 1 hour and up to 2 days.

3 MAKE THE FILLING: In a small bowl, combine the goat cheese, maple syrup, salt, and pepper. Stir to mix well.

4 MAKE THE BALSAMIC STRAWBERRIES: In a medium bowl, combine the cornstarch and balsamic vinegar. Use a fork to stir until mixed well and smooth. Add the strawberries, sugar, and salt and stir to mix well.

5 Preheat the oven to 400°F. Line a baking sheet with parchment paper.

6 Lightly flour a clean work surface. Remove the dough from the refrigerator and roll it into a 14-inch round. If it's too stiff to roll out, let it stand for 5 minutes, then try again. Transfer the dough to the prepared baking sheet; there should be some overhang. If the dough feels too soft to the touch, transfer it to the freezer to firm up slightly, 3 to 5 minutes. Add the cheese filling to the center, spreading it to the edges and leaving a 2-inch border. Top with the balsamic strawberries and any collected juices. Fold the edges of the galette dough into the center, pleating the edges to fully close it in. Brush the crust with the egg yolk. If the crust feels too soft again, place it in the freezer for 3 to 5 minutes more until mostly firm to the touch.

7 Bake the galette for 40 to 50 minutes, until the crust is deeply golden brown. Remove from the oven, then let rest for 5 minutes. Drizzle with the honey, sprinkle with the flaky salt, slice, and serve.

New York Sicilian Pizza

Serves 4 to 6

My pizza-making journey started when I was around five years old. A day with my aunt Kelly often involved her stopping at a pizza shop to ask for dough, which we'd take home to bake with our own toppings on a hot pizza stone. Those were my first experiences with freshly baked bread of any kind, and even at five years old, I could taste the awesomeness. The truth is, pizza is really hard to make at home, as many of the best styles require oven temperatures that home equipment just can't reach. But we can make thicker-style pizzas, and this one sits in the world between focaccia, grandma pies, and Sicilian slices. I've topped it lightly with ingredients from one of my favorite pastas of all time, pasta alla Norma, from Sicily. Now, if you'd like something even simpler, make this into rosemary focaccia: When the dough is in the pan and ready to be baked, drizzle 2 tablespoons extra-virgin olive oil over the top, scatter over 1 teaspoon flaky salt, and finish with 3 tablespoons fresh rosemary leaves, then bake as directed.

For the Dough

- 5 cups (700g) bread flour
- 1 (¼-ounce/7g) packet instant yeast
- 1 tablespoon kosher salt
- 3 tablespoons extra-virgin olive oil

For the Toppings

- 1 cup canned crushed tomatoes
- 4 ounces sharp provolone or fresh mozzarella cheese, cubed
- 1 tablespoon extra-virgin olive oil
- 3 tablespoons freshly grated Pecorino Romano cheese
- ¾ cup Smoky Eggplant Pesto (page 228) or store-bought pesto

1 **MAKE THE DOUGH:** In a large bowl, whisk together the bread flour and yeast. In a separate bowl, combine the salt with 3 cups of lukewarm water and stir to dissolve the salt. Add the water to the bowl with the flour and stir with a wooden spoon until there are no more dry patches of flour and a wet, loose dough forms. Cover with a clean kitchen towel and let rest for 20 minutes.

2 Once the dough has rested, grab a section of the dough, close to the edge of the bowl and pick it up, wiggle it a bit in the air to lengthen it, then stretch it across to the opposite side of the bowl. Turn the bowl one quarter turn and repeat this process 8 times, until all of the edges have been lifted and folded and the dough forms a more cohesive ball. The dough will still be very loose and fluid.

3 Coat a large, resealable container, or bowl that allows plenty of room to rise, with 2 tablespoons of the olive oil, then add the dough ball. Cover lightly with a lid or plastic wrap and place in the refrigerator for at least 24 hours and up to 72 hours.

4 A few hours before the dough is ready to be baked, add the remaining 1 tablespoon of olive oil to the bottom of a 9 × 13-inch metal baking pan. Add the dough to the pan, then using your fingers, gently dimple the dough into place to fill the entire pan. Cover tightly with plastic wrap and leave in a warm place until it has risen closer to the top of the pan, about 2 hours.

5 About 1½ hours before the second dough rise, place a baking sheet on the center rack of the oven and preheat to 500°F.

Recipe continues

6 Remove the plastic wrap from the top of the pizza and evenly spoon on the crushed tomatoes all the way to the edges of the dough. Sprinkle the provolone evenly over the top, then drizzle the olive oil.

7 Bake for 23 to 30 minutes, until the top of the pizza is blackened in a few spots, the cheese is completely melted, and the dough is cooked through. Transfer the pan to a wire rack and let cool for 5 minutes, then remove the pizza from the pan and place it on the rack until it's cool enough to handle.

8 Sprinkle the pecorino over the top, then slice the pizza into 12 pieces and add a tablespoon of the smoky eggplant dip to each slice. Serve hot or at room temperature.

French Onion Focaccia

Serves 4 to 6

I've always enjoyed discovering the flavors of dishes I love in unexpected places. I first came across the idea of merging soup and pizza in Newtown, Connecticut, at Good Old Days Pizzeria & Cocktail Den. Their French onion pizza was a familiar but totally new experience, not something I often experience when eating pizza! I had to try to make my own. How could I cram all the flavor of soup into bread without it becoming soggy? I found that cooking the onions down, then adding beef broth and finishing them slightly wet is the way to go. Handheld onion soup!

For the Dough

5 cups (700g) bread flour
1 (¼-ounce/7g) packet instant yeast
1 tablespoon kosher salt
3 tablespoons extra-virgin olive oil

For the Topping

2 tablespoons unsalted butter
1 large yellow onion, diced
½ teaspoon dried thyme
¼ teaspoon freshly ground black pepper
1 teaspoon beef bouillon paste, such as Better Than Bouillon
4 ounces Swiss cheese, cut into ¼-inch cubes

1 MAKE THE DOUGH: In a large bowl, whisk together the bread flour and yeast. In a separate bowl, combine the salt with 3 cups lukewarm water and stir to dissolve the salt. Add the water to the bowl with the flour and stir with a wooden spoon until there are no more dry patches of flour and a wet, loose dough forms. Cover with a clean kitchen towel and let rest for 20 minutes.

2 Once the dough has rested, grab a section of the dough close to the edge of the bowl and pick it up, wiggle it a bit in the air to lengthen it, then stretch it across to the opposite side of the bowl. Turn the bowl one quarter turn and repeat this process 8 times, until all of the edges have been lifted and folded and the dough forms a more cohesive ball. The dough will still be very loose and fluid.

3 Coat a large, resealable container, or bowl that allows plenty of room to rise, with 2 tablespoons of the olive oil, then add the dough ball. Cover lightly with a lid or plastic wrap and place in the refrigerator for at least 24 hours and up to 72 hours.

4 A few hours before the dough is ready to be baked, add the remaining 1 tablespoon of olive oil to the bottom of a 9 × 13-inch metal baking pan. Add the dough to the pan, then using your fingers, gently dimple the dough into place to fill the entire pan. Cover tightly with plastic wrap and leave in a warm place until it has risen closer to the top of the pan, about 2 hours.

5 About 1½ hours into the second dough rise, preheat the oven to 425°F.

6 MEANWHILE, MAKE THE TOPPING: In a medium pan, combine the butter and onion. Cover and cook over medium heat, undisturbed, until the onions are translucent and have released some moisture, about 5 minutes. Remove the lid and stir in the thyme and pepper. Cook until fragrant, about 1 minute.

Recipe continues

7 Add ½ cup water and the bouillon and stir, scraping up any browned bits from the bottom of the pan. Reduce the heat to low and cook until the onions are browned and most of the liquid has evaporated, 8 to 10 minutes. Remove from the heat and let cool.

8 Once the dough has completed its second rise, remove the plastic wrap, and with wet fingers, dimple the dough all over. Evenly scatter the caramelized onions on top, followed by the cheese.

9 Bake for 25 to 35 minutes, until the top is golden brown and the dough is cooked through. Transfer the pan to a wire rack and let cool for 5 minutes, then remove the focaccia from the pan and place it on the rack until it's cool enough to handle.

10 Slice into 12 squares. Serve hot or at room temperature. The individual slices can be wrapped in aluminum foil and frozen for up to 3 months; unwrap and reheat in a toaster oven or and air fryer at 350°F for 10 minutes.

VEGETABLES & LEGUMES

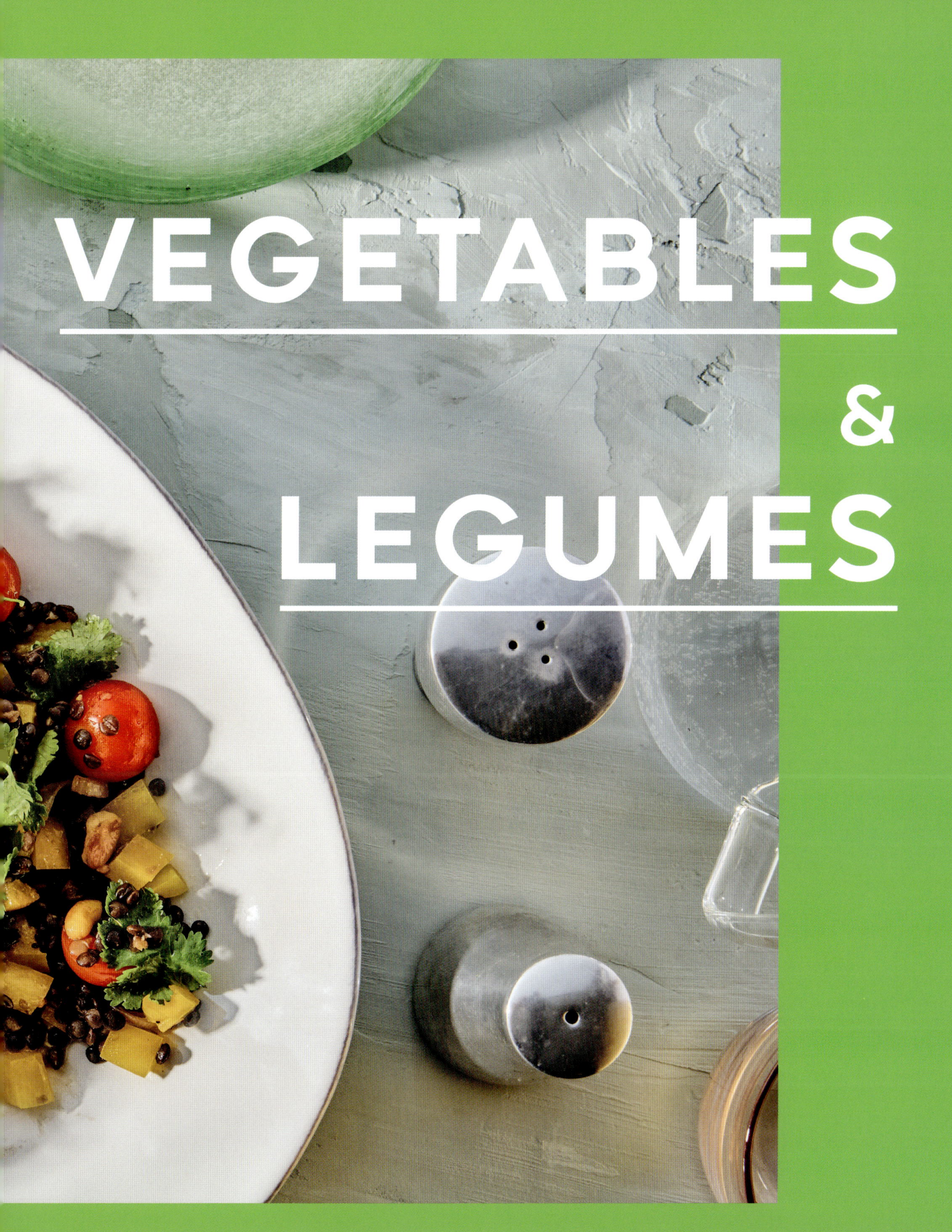

Summer Zucchini Sauté

Serves 2 as a main or 4 as a side

One of my all-time favorite summer vegetables is zucchini; it's super versatile and fast to work with, which, on a hot summer day, is a two-for-one win. When cooked quickly over high heat, zucchini holds its shape and takes on the flavors around it, making it ideal for grilling, roasting, and sautéing. In this dish, I'm using the stovetop to make the magic happen. Onions are sizzled, pine nuts toasted, red pepper flakes bloomed, basil steeped. I looked at my favorite vegetable stir-fries and asked myself, *How can I get all that speed and freshness with Mediterranean-focused ingredients?* This is that dish, and it makes a great main or side, hot or cold.

2 tablespoons extra-virgin olive oil
1 red onion, thinly sliced
2 zucchini, thinly sliced
¼ cup pine nuts
¾ teaspoon kosher salt
¼ teaspoon red pepper flakes
1 pint cherry tomatoes
¼ cup dry white wine
1 cup fresh basil leaves (about 20 medium)
½ cup shaved Parmigiano Reggiano cheese

1 In a large skillet, heat the olive oil over medium-high heat. When the oil is shimmering, add the onion and cook, stirring, until beginning to brown, 2 to 4 minutes. Add the zucchini, pine nuts, salt, and red pepper flakes. Cook, stirring occasionally, until the pine nuts just begin to turn golden and the zucchini blisters slightly, 5 to 7 minutes.

2 Add the tomatoes and pour in the wine. Increase the heat to high and cook, scraping up the browned bits from the bottom of the pan, until the alcohol has evaporated, about 1 minute. Add half the basil leaves, reduce the heat to low, and cover. Cook until the basil has wilted, about 3 minutes.

3 Remove from the heat, give everything a good stir, then top with the remaining basil and the shaved Parmigiano. Divide among plates and serve hot or at room temperature.

Roasted Broccolini

WITH PISTACHIO PARSLEY CREMA

Serves 4 as a side

Broccoli was always my favorite vegetable growing up, and when I had broccolini for the first time, it felt like an adult version of the veg I knew and loved. Longer stems and smaller florets make for a nice variety of textures that beg to be dressed. This pistachio crema turns roasted broccolini into something a little more substantial, and the slightly charred florets match really well with the crema's bright nuttiness.

For the Crema

1 (15-ounce) can cannellini beans, drained and rinsed
1 cup firmly packed fresh Italian parsley
¼ cup shelled pistachios
2 tablespoons capers, drained and rinsed
1 tablespoon fresh lemon juice
1 garlic clove, chopped
1 teaspoon Dijon mustard
¼ teaspoon kosher salt
3 tablespoons extra-virgin olive oil

For the Broccolini

3 bunches broccolini (about 1½ pounds)
3 tablespoons extra-virgin olive oil
2 tablespoons soy sauce
¼ cup Sweet & Zingy Fresno Chilies (page 230) or store-bought sliced banana peppers, plus their pickling liquid (if desired)

1 Position an oven rack 6 to 8 inches from the broiler heat source and preheat the broiler. Line a baking sheet with aluminum foil.

2 **MAKE THE CREMA:** In a high-powered blender or food processor, combine the cannellini beans, parsley, pistachios, capers, lemon juice, garlic, Dijon mustard, salt, and ½ cup cold water. Blend on low speed for about 1 minute, then increase the speed to high. Stream in the olive oil and blend until smooth, about 4 minutes.

3 **MAKE THE BROCCOLINI:** In a large bowl, combine the broccolini, olive oil, and soy sauce. Mix to coat well. Arrange the broccolini on the prepared baking sheet in a single layer. Broil for 2 to 4 minutes, until the florets just begin to char, then carefully flip them and, keeping a close eye, broil for 1 to 3 minutes more, until the second side just starts to char as well.

4 Smear the crema onto the bottom of a serving platter and arrange the broccolini on top. Top with the Fresno peppers, and for extra-bold flavor, spoon over some of the Fresnos' pickling liquid. Serve.

Asparagus & Cheese

Serves 4 as a side

Nonno Frank made me the classic French version of this for lunch one spring day in 2000. I think he was in the process of overhauling his kitchen, because I remember eating and preparing the dish in a makeshift kitchen in the basement. Since he didn't have his dedicated broiler, it was the first time I ever saw someone use a blowtorch in the kitchen. It's something that stuck with me ever since. This dish is cooked all at once, and at the very end, the broiler is activated to brûlée the cheese and breadcrumbs.

- 2 bunches asparagus (about 2 pounds total), trimmed
- 3 tablespoons extra-virgin olive oil
- ½ cup panko breadcrumbs
- ¾ cup packed freshly grated Jarlsberg cheese
- ¼ cup freshly grated Parmigiano Reggiano cheese
- ¼ cup whole milk
- ¼ teaspoon kosher salt
- ¼ teaspoon freshly ground black pepper
- ¼ teaspoon granulated garlic
- 2 Cured Egg Yolks (page 233), or an additional 2 tablespoons freshly grated Parmigiano Reggiano cheese

1 Position a rack in the top third of the oven and preheat to 400°F. Line a rimmed baking sheet with parchment paper.

2 Arrange the asparagus in a single layer on the prepared baking sheet and drizzle with 1 tablespoon of the olive oil.

3 In a medium bowl, stir together the panko, Jarlsberg, Parmigiano, milk, the remaining 2 tablespoons olive oil, the salt, pepper, and granulated garlic. Spread the breadcrumb mixture on top of the asparagus, being sure to avoid their tips.

4 Roast for 15 minutes, then turn on the broiler and broil, keeping a watchful eye on the asparagus, for about 2 minutes, until beautiful brown spots begin to appear. Remove from the oven.

5 Using a Microplane, grate half a cured egg yolk onto each portion and serve.

Roasted Carrots

WITH SMOKY CASHEW "CREAM"

Serves 4 to 6 as a side

My mother-in-law, Lynne, eats plant-based, and while she's happy with in-season raw ingredients, quinoa, and vinaigrettes, I always try to make her something that feels a little bit more substantial. This is one of those dishes, and I'm happy to say that she loves the "decadence." Cashews are soaked in water, then blended to an almost queso-like consistency. When mixed with smoked paprika, the roasted carrots almost taste like something you'd get at a BBQ joint: rich, in-your-face, and extra flavorful. I don't peel my carrots—I just wash them well—but either way is fine.

For the Cashew Cream

½ cup whole raw cashews
1 garlic clove
1 teaspoon kosher salt
1 teaspoon smoked paprika
½ teaspoon ground cumin
1 teaspoon sherry vinegar
1 tablespoon fresh lemon juice

For the Carrots

2 bunches carrots (about 2 pounds), stems trimmed to 1 inch long
2 tablespoons extra-virgin olive oil
½ teaspoon kosher salt
¼ teaspoon freshly ground black pepper

For Serving

1 head Roasted Garlic (page 230)
¼ cup Pan-Fried Breadcrumbs (page 231) or store-bought seasoned breadcrumbs
Honey
Flaky salt

1 Preheat the oven to 400°F. Line a baking sheet with parchment paper.

2 MAKE THE CASHEW CREAM: Fill a small pot with 3 cups water and bring to a boil over high heat. Remove from the heat and add the cashews. Let soak for 20 minutes.

3 Drain the cashews and transfer them to a high-powered blender or food processor. Add ½ cup water, the garlic, salt, paprika, cumin, vinegar, and lemon juice. Blend on low speed for 30 seconds, then increase the speed to high and blend until smooth, 1 to 2 minutes. Add up to ½ cup more water if needed to reach the desired consistency.

4 MEANWHILE, MAKE THE CARROTS: On the prepared baking sheet, combine the carrots, olive oil, salt, and pepper. Toss to coat well. Roast the carrots for 30 minutes, or until tender but still slightly resistant when poked with a knife. Transfer to a serving platter.

5 Drizzle the cashew cream over the carrots, dollop on the roasted garlic cloves, and scatter the breadcrumbs over the top. Drizzle with honey and finish with flaky salt before serving.

Bright Black Lentil Salad

Serves 4 to 6

In my private cheffing days, I was always loved to place a variation of this lentil salad down on the table. Visually, it's beautiful, with vibrant summer produce that pops against the contrast of the deep black lentils. It's delicious, too, fresh and clean, and there's no worry of the flavors expiring quickly. This makes it perfect at room temp on a summer day, and a great choice for picnics or (less fun) bring-to-work lunches. It's endlessly customizable, and I'm sure you'll make it your own in no time.

For the Salad

1 cup dried black lentils
1 bay leaf
1 yellow bell pepper, diced
1 pint cherry tomatoes, halved
1 cup fresh cilantro
2 tablespoons extra-virgin olive oil
¼ teaspoon plus ⅛ teaspoon kosher salt
1 large shallot, sliced
¼ cup raw cashews
¼ teaspoon freshly ground black pepper

For the Dressing

1 tablespoon extra-virgin olive oil
1 tablespoon sherry vinegar
½ teaspoon Dijon mustard
¼ teaspoon kosher salt

1 MAKE THE SALAD: In a medium saucepan, combine the lentils, bay leaf, and 2 cups water and bring to a boil over high heat. Reduce the heat to low, cover, and simmer until the lentils are cooked through but still hold their shape, about 20 minutes. Remove and discard the bay leaf. Drain the lentils in a fine-mesh sieve and rinse until the water runs clear and the lentils are cool.

2 Transfer the lentils to a large bowl and add the bell pepper, tomatoes, cilantro, 1 tablespoon of the olive oil, and ¼ teaspoon salt. Stir to mix well.

3 In a small skillet, heat the remaining 1 tablespoon olive oil over medium-high heat. When the oil is shimmering, add the shallot, cashews, the remaining ⅛ teaspoon salt, and the black pepper. Cook until about half the shallots begin to char and the cashews are just a few shades darker, about 3 minutes. Add to the bowl with the lentils and stir to mix well.

4 MAKE THE DRESSING: In a small lidded jar, combine the olive oil, vinegar, Dijon, and salt. Seal the jar and shake well until emulsified.

5 Pour the dressing over the lentils and toss to coat well. Serve family-style in a large shallow bowl. Store leftovers in an airtight container in the refrigerator for up to 2 days.

Brothy, Spicy Ruffage & Beans

Serves 4

This dish not quite a soup, but it's way juicier than sautéed greens. I guess you could say it lives somewhere in the middle—and it's good hot or cold, as a main or in support of roasted fish or chicken. The slight bitterness of the escarole is balanced by the sweetness of slowly cooked onions and fennel. If you want to make it even more substantial, swap the escarole for purple cabbage and cook it a few minutes longer.

2 tablespoons extra-virgin olive oil
1 fennel bulb, thinly sliced, fronds reserved
1 yellow onion, thinly sliced
3 garlic cloves, smashed and peeled
1½ teaspoons fennel seed, crushed
1 teaspoon red pepper flakes
1½ teaspoons kosher salt, plus more as needed
1 large or 2 small heads escarole, leaves separated and torn into large pieces
1 (15-ounce) can cannellini beans, drained and rinsed
3 cups low-sodium vegetable broth
1 teaspoon Calabrian chili paste
2 tablespoons goat cheese

1 In a large Dutch oven, heat the olive oil over medium-high heat. When the oil is shimmering, add the sliced fennel, onion, garlic, fennel seed, red pepper flakes, and 1 teaspoon of the salt. Cook, stirring occasionally, until the onion and fennel begin to turn golden, about 10 minutes. Add the escarole and cook, stirring, until it has wilted and the moisture evaporates, about 3 minutes.

2 Add the cannellini beans, broth, and remaining ½ teaspoon salt. Increase the heat to high and bring to a boil, then remove from the heat. Taste and adjust the salt as needed.

3 Divide the greens and beans among bowls. Top each bowl evenly with the chili paste, goat cheese, and fennel fronds and serve.

LE C

Roasted Baby Potatoes

WITH ZINGY ROMESCO SAUCE

Serves 4 to 6 as a side

There was a period in my private cheffing days when I was both obsessed with Spanish pimentón (smoked paprika) and cooking entire meals over a wood fire. Taking inspiration from the bold flavors of Spain, I'd riff off their simple classics—ingredients that would be fried, I'd fire roast—and I came up with this dish as a nod to patatas bravas: salty, oily potatoes cooked hard, served with a vinegary, in-your-face romesco that can be whipped up in a blender in no time. It's an intense combination that's very bright, which pairs well with hearty meat and fish dishes.

- 1½ pounds baby Yukon Gold potatoes, halved if large
- ⅓ cup extra-virgin olive oil
- 1½ teaspoons kosher salt
- ½ teaspoon freshly ground black pepper
- 1½ cups romesco sauce, homemade (page 226) or store-bought

1 Preheat the oven to 450°F.

2 On a baking sheet, combine the potatoes, olive oil, and salt. Toss to coat well. Turn any halved potatoes cut-side down. Roast the potatoes for 30 minutes, or until fork-tender. Remove the baking sheet from the oven. Add the pepper and toss to coat. Turn any halved potatoes cut-side up. Roast for 5 minutes more, until the pepper is aromatic.

3 Remove from the oven and gently shake the tray to cover the potatoes in any remaining oil and spices. Let cool for 10 to 15 minutes, then transfer the potatoes to a serving bowl. Add 1 cup of the romesco sauce and toss to coat well (my preferred way to enjoy these), or serve with the sauce on the side.

4 Serve the potatoes with more romesco sauce to taste.

Couscous-Stuffed Peppers

Makes 18 to 24 bites

When I search the internet for stuffed peppers, not one photo looks like the version I grew up eating. In fact, they all look the same: The top of the pepper is cut off, the cavity is filled with all kinds of things, and then the top is replaced. Call me crazy, but I find this boring, and way too much of a commitment—a whole pepper plus all the fillings is likely a full pound of food, which doesn't leave much room for other dishes. The peppers I enjoyed as a kid, made by my grandparents on my dad's side, were delicate and edible in two bites. While these do require some hands-on time, the steps are easy and repetitive, and for me, the result is worth it.

6 red bell peppers
3 tablespoons extra-virgin olive oil
1 cup couscous (not Israeli couscous)
2 tablespoons raisins
1 tablespoon balsamic vinegar
1 cup chopped fresh parsley
1 cup freshly grated Parmigiano Reggiano cheese
¼ cup pine nuts
1 (6-ounce) can pitted black olives, drained and chopped
2 garlic cloves, chopped
½ teaspoon kosher salt, plus more if needed
½ teaspoon freshly ground black pepper
1 large egg, beaten

1 Position a rack in the center of the oven and preheat to 400°F. Line a baking sheet with parchment paper.

2 Stand each pepper upright and cut it in half, cutting straight down through the stem. Remove the seeds and any excess white bits. Place the peppers cut-side down on the prepared baking sheet. Add 1 tablespoon of the olive oil and rub it all over the peppers.

3 Roast the peppers for 25 minutes, or until dark spots begin to appear. Immediately transfer the roasted peppers to a large bowl and cover tightly with plastic wrap (leave the oven on and reserve the baking sheet). Let steam for about 10 minutes, or until cool enough to handle. Peel the peppers and discard the skin. Use a paring knife to cut between the vertical running ribs of each pepper to create 3 or 4 small boats per pepper.

4 Meanwhile, fill a medium pot with 1¼ cups water and bring to a boil over high heat. Remove from the heat and add the couscous, raisins, and balsamic vinegar. Give the pot a swirl, cover, then set aside to steam and infuse for 5 minutes. Remove the lid and add the parsley, cheese, pine nuts, olives, garlic, remaining 2 tablespoons olive oil, the salt, and the black pepper. Mix well, taste, and add more salt if needed. Add the egg and mix well to combine.

5 Working with one pepper piece at a time, stuff the pepper boats with the filling, dividing it evenly. Place each boat stuffed-side down on the prepared baking sheet.

6 Roast for about 10 minutes, until the edges of the pepper just begin to brown and the egg has cooked through. Remove and let rest for at least 5 minutes before enjoying. Store in an airtight container in the refrigerator for 2 days.

In-Your-Face Tomato Salad

Serves 4 as a side

Tomatoes are incredibly, mind-blowingly awesome for exactly two weeks each year in the Northeast. When they're at their peak, they need nothing added—it's perfection. Bites like these make me wonder, *What is cooking? What is a recipe?* But this flavor nirvana is brief where I live, and this salad is my attempt at forcing umami and funk into the tomatoes that are available the other fifty weeks of the year. Parsley or celery leaves go a long way in adding freshness to balance the umami richness. Any leftover marinade can be enjoyed with bread, as a flavoring for rice, or to enhance the potatoes that go with the roasted chicken on page 138.

- 2 tablespoons low-sodium soy sauce
- 2 tablespoons extra-virgin olive oil
- 1 teaspoon sugar
- 1 teaspoon fish sauce
- 1 teaspoon sherry vinegar
- 1 garlic clove, minced
- 1 Thai bird's-eye chili, chopped, or ¼ teaspoon red pepper flakes
- ⅛ teaspoon kosher salt
- ¼ teaspoon freshly ground black pepper
- 1½ pounds heirloom tomatoes (about 3 large), cut into 1-inch-thick wedges
- Fresh parsley or celery leaves, for garnish

1 In a medium bowl, combine the soy sauce, olive oil, sugar, fish sauce, vinegar, garlic, chili, salt, and black pepper. Whisk to combine well and fully dissolve the sugar. Add the tomato wedges and gently toss to coat. Let the tomatoes marinate at room temperature for at least 15 minutes or up to an hour, tossing a few times throughout.

2 Use a slotted spoon to transfer the tomatoes to a serving platter. Pour half the excess marinade over the top, then garnish with parsley or celery leaves.

Giant Cheesy Tot

Serves 4 as a side

Now that I have your attention, behold: a delicious potato and cheese pie! This dish is somewhere between a Swiss rösti, a delicious giant potato pancake, and Friulan frico, which uses potato and onion to hold together what is effectively a melted cheese treat. I love both of those regional specialties. The shreds of potato fry, steam, and bake all at the same time, creating a multitextural experience that excites! Better yet, making one giant tot is way easier than making one hundred of them. Use a super-smooth carbon-steel pan or a nonstick pan to get this job done well.

1 medium russet potato (about 10 ounces), peeled and grated on the large holes of a box grater
1 tablespoon unsalted butter
2 garlic cloves, grated
5 ounces Jarlsberg cheese, cut into ¼-inch cubes
½ teaspoon kosher salt
1 tablespoon fresh thyme leaves (from about 4 sprigs)

1 Transfer the grated potato to a clean kitchen towel and, holding it over the sink, squeeze out as much liquid as possible. Transfer the potato to a large bowl.

2 Melt the butter in an 8-inch nonstick skillet over medium heat. Add the garlic and cook until fragrant, 1 to 2 minutes. Add half the cheese, followed by the potato, salt, and thyme, then add the remaining cheese. Using a rubber spatula, mix from bottom to top until fully combined, 1 to 3 minutes. Let the cheese melt, undisturbed (it will sound like an active fireplace), for another 6 minutes or so. Work the spatula around the edges, pushing inward toward the center, reducing the circumference of the mass and separating the ingredients from the pan, then swirl the pan; the ingredients should be totally free from sticking to the pan.

3 Place a large plate on top of the skillet and invert the pan to release the tot. Return the flipped tot to the pan and cook until the second side is golden brown as well, about 5 minutes more. Using the spatula, continue to "round" the edges of the tot as it cooks, occasionally ensuring nothing is sticking to the pan.

4 When both sides are deeply golden brown, transfer the tot to a plate, let cool for 5 minutes, then cut into 4 pieces and serve.

Broccoli Rabe Tonnato

Serves 4 as a side

I'm on a quest to make more people love broccoli rabe. Too often I see people sauté it right out of the gate, which is a mistake! Quickly blanching broccoli rabe in salted boiling water before sautéing seriously mellows its classic bitterness, which makes all the difference. But for those who still find it too bitter, I present to you: broccoli rabe tonnato. Think of tonnato as a briny, sweet, very light tuna aioli, traditionally served atop thinly sliced veal in Italian cuisine. As with veal and tuna, broccoli rabe and tuna might sound odd, but in both instances, the combination tastes great!

For the Tonnato

- 1 (6.7-ounce) jar tuna packed in water, drained
- ½ cup mayonnaise
- 3 oil-packed anchovy fillets
- ¼ cup extra-virgin olive oil
- 2 tablespoons fresh lemon juice
- 1 tablespoon drained capers

For the Broccoli Rabe

- 2 tablespoons kosher salt
- 3 bunches broccoli rabe (about 2½ pounds total)
- 3 tablespoons extra-virgin olive oil
- 5 garlic cloves, smashed and peeled
- 1 teaspoon red pepper flakes

1 MAKE THE TONNATO: In a high-powered blender or food processor, combine the tuna, mayonnaise, anchovies, olive oil, lemon juice, and capers. Blend on medium-low speed until smooth, about 1 minute.

2 MAKE THE BROCCOLI RABE: Fill a large saucepan with 4 quarts water and bring to a boil over high heat. Add the salt and the broccoli rabe and cook, stirring gently, until bright green, about 4 minutes. Drain the broccoli rabe and rinse with cool water for 1 minute to stop the cooking.

3 Wipe out the pan, then heat the olive oil over medium-high heat. When the oil is shimmering, tilt the pan away from you so the oil pools in the far edge, then drop in the garlic so it's fully submerged. When the garlic begins to brown, about 1 minute, add the red pepper flakes, set the pan back down flat on the stove, and turn off the heat. Immediately add the blanched broccoli rabe and vigorously toss it in the oil until the sizzling has subsided and the oil has been mostly absorbed, 3 to 5 minutes.

4 Pour half the tonnato onto a serving platter and arrange the broccoli rabe and garlic cloves on top. Drizzle any remaining oil from the pan over the broccoli rabe and finish with the remaining tonnato. Serve.

BEEF & LAMB

Thai-Style Beef Salad

Serves 2 as a main or 4 as a starter

Head to a quality Thai restaurant, and you'll find laab (or larb) on the menu. Whenever I'm trying out a new place, this dish is my point of reference. It's a simple salad often made with beef, chicken, duck, or pork. I've never had two that were prepared the same way; sometimes they're served cold, other times warm; sometimes the acidity is extra pronounced, other times chefs push the boundaries of the spiciness to cut through the richness of a fattier meat. I love the variety, and I love taking inspiration from them all and trying my hand at making it at home.

- 1 pound 80% lean ground beef
- 1 teaspoon kosher salt
- 1 teaspoon sugar
- ¾ cup chopped mixed fresh herbs, such as basil, cilantro, mint, and/or parsley
- 4 scallions, chopped
- ¼ cup toasted rice powder (see Note)
- ¼ cup fresh lime juice (from about 3 limes)
- 2 tablespoons chopped Sweet & Zingy Fresno Chilies (page 230) or store-bought sliced pickled banana peppers, plus 2 tablespoons pickling liquid
- 1 tablespoon fish sauce
- ¼ teaspoon chili powder
- 8 to 12 red lettuce leaves

1 In a medium skillet, combine the beef, salt, sugar, and ¼ cup water. Bring to a gentle simmer over medium heat and cook, breaking up the beef with a wooden spoon, until cooked through and no longer pink, about 5 minutes. Use a slotted spoon to transfer the beef to a medium bowl.

2 Add the fresh herbs, scallions, rice powder, lime juice, Fresno chilies and pickling liquid, fish sauce, and chili powder to the bowl with the beef. Stir to combine well. Taste and adjust the seasoning as needed.

3 Divide the lettuce among plates, top with the beef, and enjoy.

NOTE: A key ingredient for staying faithful to the original dish is toasted rice powder. It thickens, adds texture, and brings a welcome nuttiness to the dish. If you're unable to find it at the store, just toast ½ cup uncooked jasmine rice (or even white quinoa) in a skillet over medium-high heat, stirring frequently, until fragrant. Let it cool, then pulverize it into a powder in a high-powered blender.

Mediterranean Steak

Serves 4

As a ten-year-old, I wouldn't touch raw fish, but I had no problem eating carpaccio di manzo, an Italian raw beef salad with olive oil and lemon. To make a great one, you need a meat slicer and a big, clean area where you can pound the meat thinly, so I set out to simplify it. For my friends who are afraid of raw beef, I'll share this tidbit that I learned in culinary school: Whole pieces of meat are sterile inside. A quick sear here adds a little flavor, but it also kills off any microbes. Because you're not cooking the meat through, there should be no juices at all when you cut into it. The lemon dressing is a trick from the ceviche playbook; the acid in the lemon juice cooks the meat ever so slightly and doubles down on the crisp, clean flavors.

For the Steak

1 pound filet mignon
1 teaspoon neutral oil
½ teaspoon kosher salt
1 teaspoon freshly ground black pepper

For the Salad

5 ounces arugula
4 tablespoons lemon dressing, homemade (page 225) or store-bought
¼ teaspoon freshly ground black pepper

For Serving

1 cup shaved Parmigiano Reggiano cheese
¼ teaspoon flaky salt
Sweet & Zingy Fresno Chilies (page 230), plus some of their pickling liquid, or store-bought sliced pickled banana peppers (optional)

1 **MAKE THE STEAK:** Pat the steak dry. Rub it all over with the neutral oil, then season with salt and pepper.

2 Heat a medium cast-iron skillet over medium-high heat for about 2 minutes. Place the steak in the pan and cook until just browned on the outside, about 2 minutes per side. Transfer the steak to a paper towel–lined plate, pat off any excess oil, then transfer to a cutting board and slice as thinly as possible. Divide the steak among four plates.

3 **MAKE THE SALAD:** In a medium bowl, combine the arugula, 2 tablespoons of the lemon dressing, and the pepper. Toss to coat well, then divide the salad among the plates with the steak.

4 Spoon the remaining 2 tablespoons dressing over the steaks, then sprinkle on the Parmigiano shavings and the flaky salt. Add some Fresno chilies and a drizzle of their pickling liquid, if you'd like, and serve.

Lamb Meatballs

WITH GARLICKY YOGURT

Serves 4

Once you realize that meatballs are a form factor not exclusive to Italian cuisine, the culinary possibilities for improvisation expand immensely. I crave traditional Middle Eastern lamb kofta, but I can't always make it. These meatballs allow me to capture that big taste I love in another way. Here, sweet raisins, cumin, garlic, and herbs combine to create an explosion of strong, fresh flavors that will keep you coming back for more. A cooling yogurt sauce accompanies the meatballs to provide some flavor contrast and temperature variance.

For the Lamb Meatballs

1 tablespoon extra-virgin olive oil
¼ cup chopped raisins
¼ cup chopped fresh mint leaves
¼ cup chopped fresh cilantro
¼ cup breadcrumbs, plus more if needed
2 garlic cloves, grated
1 large egg
2 teaspoons ground cumin
½ teaspoon red pepper flakes
1½ teaspoons kosher salt
½ teaspoon freshly ground black pepper
1 pound ground lamb

For the Yogurt Sauce

1 cup plain full-fat yogurt
1 garlic clove, grated
1 teaspoon sherry vinegar
⅛ teaspoon kosher salt

1 **MAKE THE MEATBALLS:** Preheat the oven to 425°F. Drizzle olive oil over a baking sheet.

2 Place the raisins in a medium bowl and pour ¼ cup warm water over the top. Push the raisins down to submerge them, if needed, and set aside to soak until plump and lighter in color, about 2 minutes. Add the mint, cilantro, breadcrumbs, garlic, egg, cumin, red pepper flakes, salt, and black pepper and whisk to combine. Let stand until the breadcrumbs soften, about 2 minutes.

3 Add the lamb and use your hands to gently combine, taking care not to overwork. The mixture should be wet, but just sticky enough to form a ball. If there's too much moisture, add 1 tablespoon of breadcrumbs. Form the mixture into golf ball–size meatballs and place them on the prepared baking sheet. You should have about 16 meatballs.

4 Bake for about 10 minutes, until the bottoms of the meatballs are browned. Flip each meatball over and bake for 10 minutes more, until browned on the second side.

5 **MEANWHILE, MAKE THE YOGURT SAUCE:** In a small bowl, combine the yogurt, garlic, vinegar, and salt.

6 Arrange the meatballs on a serving platter and serve with the yogurt sauce on the side.

Spicy Beef Dip

Makes 4 (6-inch) sandwiches

Since I was a kid, I've always loved a good French dip: crusty bread, flavorful beef, and juicy dipping sauce. It's a great sandwich, and one could argue nothing about it needs to change. But I can't sit still, and I love combining my favorite dishes. That's why I've added a few elements from birria, a Jalisco-style Mexican stew, my favorite variation of which is served as a griddled taco. The experience of my spicy beef dip is extra flavorful, fun, and relaxed, if a little messy.

1½ pounds top sirloin, 1¼ to 2 inches thick
1 teaspoon kosher salt
1 teaspoon freshly ground black pepper
1 tablespoon neutral oil
1 white onion, diced
3 canned chipotle peppers in adobo sauce
½ teaspoon ground cumin
¼ cup balsamic vinegar
2 teaspoons beef bouillon paste, such as Better Than Bouillon
1 (24-inch-long) baguette
8 ounces pepper Jack cheese, sliced

For Serving

½ cup fresh cilantro leaves
Flaky salt
Sweet & Zingy Fresno Chilies (page 230) or store-bought sliced pickled banana peppers (optional)
Lime wedges

1 Position a rack in the upper third of the oven and preheat to 250°F. Set a wire rack over a baking sheet.

2 Pat the steak dry. Season on both sides with salt and pepper. In a large Dutch oven, heat the oil over high heat. When the oil is shimmering, add the steak. Cook until a nice brown crust forms, 3 to 4 minutes per side.

3 Transfer the steak to the prepared rack (reserve the Dutch oven) and roast until an instant-read thermometer inserted into the thickest part reaches 130°F, 25 to 35 minutes, depending on the thickness. Remove from the oven and let rest for 5 minutes, then thinly slice the steak against the grain. Turn the oven to broil.

4 Meanwhile, in the Dutch oven you used to cook the steak, combine half the onion, the chipotles, and cumin. Cook over medium-low heat, stirring occasionally, until the spices are fragrant and the onions have softened, about 5 minutes. Add the balsamic vinegar and stir, scraping up any browned bits from the bottom of the pot. Add 3 cups water and the bouillon paste, plus the remaining onions. Bring to a simmer to dissolve the paste, reduce the heat to low, and cover the pot to keep warm and infuse.

5 Set a wire rack over a baking sheet. Cut the baguette in half crosswise, then split each half horizontally. Place all four pieces cut-side up on the prepared rack. Scatter the cheese evenly across all four slices. Broil for 1 to 3 minutes, until the cheese is completely melted.

6 Lay the sliced steak on the bottom pieces of the bread. Top with cilantro, flaky salt, and Fresno peppers, if desired. Close up the sandwiches, then slice them in half on a diagonal. Serve each sandwich with a lime wedge for squeezing and ¾ cup of the broth for dipping. Be sure to dip every single bite in the broth for maximum juiciness and joy.

Spiced Roasted Lamb & Zhoug Orzo

Serves 4 to 6

In the internet age, sometimes we find things we didn't know we were searching for—and that's how I learned about zhoug. In simplified terms, it's a Yemeni hot sauce that's almost like the very spiced, cilantro-based cousin to chimichurri—bright, fresh, and in-your-face. I mix the zhoug with orzo to make a counterpoint and complementary side to the lamb, which is bold, rich, and meaty. The result is a balanced, knock-your-socks-off meal.

For the Lamb

3 tablespoons tomato paste
3 tablespoons Dijon mustard
1 tablespoon adobo seasoning (see Note)
2 teaspoons kosher salt
1 (2¼-pound) boneless leg of lamb

For the Orzo

1½ teaspoons kosher salt
1¼ cups dried orzo
1½ teaspoons extra-virgin olive oil

For the Zhoug

½ teaspoon coriander seeds
¼ teaspoon cardamom seeds
¼ teaspoon caraway seeds
½ teaspoon kosher salt, plus more if needed
½ teaspoon freshly ground black pepper
½ teaspoon red pepper flakes
¼ teaspoon ground cumin
¼ cup extra-virgin olive oil
¼ cup fresh lemon juice, plus more if needed
1 bunch cilantro, very finely chopped
2 garlic cloves, very finely chopped
1½ teaspoons honey, plus more if needed

1 **MAKE THE LAMB:** Position a rack in the lower third of the oven and preheat to 425°F. Line a baking sheet with aluminum foil.

2 In a small bowl, stir together the tomato paste, Dijon, adobo seasoning, and salt. Coat the lamb all over, inside and out, with the rub. Place it on the prepared baking sheet and roast until an instant-read thermometer inserted into the thickest part of the meat reaches 145°F, about 1 hour (25 minutes per pound). Remove from the oven and let rest for 10 to 15 minutes.

3 **MEANWHILE, MAKE THE ORZO:** Fill a medium pot with 2 quarts water and bring to a boil over high heat. Add 1½ teaspoons salt and the orzo. Cook according to the package instructions, then drain. Return the orzo to the hot pot and stir in the olive oil.

4 **MAKE THE ZHOUG:** In a mortar or spice grinder, combine the coriander, cardamom, and caraway. Mash with the pestle or pulse until ground, then transfer to a large bowl and stir in the salt, black pepper, red pepper flakes, and cumin. Add the olive oil, lemon juice, cilantro, garlic, and honey and mix well to combine. Taste—if it's flat, add more salt, lemon juice, or both; if it's too bitter, add a little more honey.

5 Add the orzo to the bowl with the zhoug and stir to combine. Slice the lamb into 1-inch-thick pieces and serve with the orzo.

NOTE: If you don't have adobo seasoning, combine 1 teaspoon sweet paprika, 1 teaspoon cayenne pepper, 1 teaspoon ground cumin, and ½ teaspoon granulated garlic and use that instead.

Moussaka

Serves 4 to 6

I had my first bike of moussaka with my dad at a Greek restaurant in Hell's Kitchen. He pointed to it on the menu and said, "Moussaka is delicious." A huge fan of eggplant Parmigiana and shepherd's pie, he described it as something of a combination. My version, which forgoes potatoes, is inspired by the Greek interpretation of a dish that has a long history in the Baltic states and the Middle East. It's hearty, savory, sweet, and well loved.

For the Eggplant

- 1 medium eggplant, sliced lengthwise into ¼-inch-thick planks
- 3 tablespoons extra-virgin olive oil
- 1 teaspoon kosher salt

For the Meat Sauce

- 2 tablespoons extra-virgin olive oil
- 1 large yellow onion, diced
- 1 teaspoon kosher salt
- 1 teaspoon freshly ground black pepper
- 12 ounces shiitake mushrooms, chopped
- 2 pounds 80% lean ground beef
- 2 teaspoons dried thyme
- 2 teaspoons ground cinnamon
- 1 teaspoon ground allspice
- 1 (15-ounce) can crushed tomatoes

For the Cheese Sauce

- 4 tablespoons (½ stick) unsalted butter
- 5 tablespoons all-purpose flour
- 2 cups whole milk
- 3 large eggs
- ½ cup grated Parmigiano Reggiano cheese (grated on the large holes of a box grater)

1 **MAKE THE EGGPLANT:** Preheat the oven to 400°F (see Note). Set a wire rack over a baking sheet.

2 Brush both sides of the eggplant slices with the olive oil. Arrange them in a single layer on the prepared rack and season with the salt. Roast for 25 to 30 minutes, until dark brown around the edges. Remove from the oven and reduce the oven temperature to 350°F.

3 **MAKE THE MEAT SAUCE:** In a large Dutch oven, heat the olive oil over medium heat. When the oil is shimmering, add the onion, salt, and pepper. Cook, stirring occasionally, until the onion is translucent, about 8 minutes. Add the mushrooms, stir, then cook, undisturbed, until they have released all their liquid and just begun to fry, 5 to 8 minutes.

4 Add the beef, thyme, cinnamon, and allspice. Increase the heat to high and cook, breaking up the meat with a wooden spoon, until cooked through and no longer pink, 8 to 10 minutes. Add the tomatoes and bring to a boil, then reduce the heat to low and simmer until the sauce thickens, about 5 minutes more.

5 **MEANWHILE, MAKE THE CHEESE SAUCE:** In a small saucepan, melt the butter over medium heat. Add the flour and cook, whisking, until no lumps remain, about 2 minutes. Add about one-third of the milk, then cook, whisking vigorously, until the sauce thickens. Repeat with another third of the milk, then again with the remainder, 3 to 5 minutes total.

6 In a medium bowl, beat the eggs. While whisking continuously, slowly pour in about one-third of the hot milk mixture. Wait about 30 seconds, then whisk in the remaining milk mixture in two more additions. Stir in the Parmigiano to melt and combine.

7 To assemble, arrange the eggplant in a single layer in a 9 × 13-inch baking dish. Add the meat. If any eggplant slices remain, use them to make another layer. Pour the cheese sauce over the top. Cover with aluminum foil and bake for 40 minutes, then uncover; the cheese sauce will have puffed up. Bake, uncovered, for 15 minutes more, or until a few brown spots appear. Remove from the oven and let cool for 15 minutes before slicing and serving.

NOTE: If your oven has a convection mode, use that, and cook the eggplant at 375°F. Alternatively, if you have an air fryer, use that—just be sure to give the slices of eggplant space between each other.

Vinegar-Braised Short Ribs

Serves 4 to 6

A braise is basically a fancy stew; the difference is that less liquid is used in a braise and the meat is never fully submerged. The vinegar in the dish mellows out significantly, adding a sweet acidy to an otherwise very rich dish. The braising is done with no lid, a trick I learned from culinary producer Rachel Dolfi, and one that made me exclaim, "Why didn't I think of that?!" This trick yields a perfectly reduced sauce that is a result of the cooking, not an added step tacked on at the end. Prepare yourself for the majesty of fall-off-the-bone short ribs!

For the Short Ribs

- 3 pounds bone-in beef short ribs
- ½ teaspoon kosher salt, plus more as needed
- 1 small yellow onion, minced
- 10 garlic cloves, smashed and peeled
- ¼ cup distilled white vinegar
- ¼ cup sherry vinegar
- 2 cups low-sodium beef broth
- 1 tablespoon light or dark brown sugar
- ½ teaspoon freshly ground black pepper, plus more as needed
- 2 bay leaves

For the Mashed Potatoes and Celery Root

- 1 pound Yukon Gold potatoes, peeled and cubed
- 1 pound celery root, peeled and cut into ½-inch-thick sticks
- 1½ teaspoons kosher salt
- 3 tablespoons unsalted butter
- ½ cup whole milk
- ½ teaspoon freshly ground black pepper

1 **MAKE THE SHORT RIBS:** Season the short ribs all over with salt, then place half in a large Dutch oven. Cook over medium-high heat until golden brown on the bottom, about 5 minutes, then flip and cook until the second side is golden brown, about 2 minutes more. Turn and brown the last non-bone side, about 2 more minutes. Transfer the ribs to a plate and repeat with the remaining short ribs, reducing the heat as needed.

2 Reduce the heat to medium-low, add the onion, and stir to combine with the rendered fat left in the pot. Cover and cook until the edges of the onion begin to soften and turn translucent, about 2 minutes. Remove the lid, add the garlic, and cook until golden brown around the edges, 6 to 8 minutes.

3 Add the white and sherry vinegars and stir, scraping up any browned bits from the bottom of the pan. Add the short ribs and any juices that have collected on the plate, the broth, brown sugar, pepper, and bay leaves and bring to a gentle simmer. Cook, uncovered, maintaining the gentlest simmer possible, until the short ribs are fork-tender, about 3 hours.

4 **ABOUT 20 MINUTES BEFORE THE SHORT RIBS ARE DONE, MAKE THE MASH:** In a large saucepan, combine the potatoes, celery root, and salt. Add water to cover the vegetables by 1 inch, cover the pan, and bring to a boil over high heat. Reduce the heat to maintain a hard simmer and cook until the vegetables are fork-tender, about 15 minutes. Drain, then return the vegetables to the hot saucepan and cook over low heat, stirring frequently, until most of the moisture has evaporated and the potatoes look chalky, about 1 minute. Remove from the heat and add the butter and milk. Using a potato masher, mash the potatoes and celery root together until they have a textured but mostly creamy consistency. Taste and season with more salt and pepper, if needed.

5 Divide the mash among bowls, then top with the short ribs. Serve immediately.

Choripan

Makes 4 sandwiches

In January 2018, I went to Argentina for the first time, and one of goals during that visit was to find the best choripan in the city. Choripan, a chorizo and chimichurri sandwich, can be found all over Buenos Aires—or so I was told. Because there are so few ingredients, the bread can make or break it. Like a New Orleans po'boy, the bread should be sturdy on the outside but light as a feather inside. I searched alone for over an hour, but I eventually had places to be and had to abandon my quest for the time being. Lucky for me, the film crew I was working with told me the best spot was around the corner. And so after work, we all had choripan and beers, the ideal beverage for what I consider one of the most satisfying sandwiches in the world. If you have access to high-quality fresh chorizo, by all means, use it to make the chorizo patties!

For the Chorizo Patties

1 pound ground pork
3 tablespoons chopped garlic
2 teaspoons tomato paste
2 tablespoons sweet paprika
1 teaspoon smoked paprika
1 teaspoon kosher salt
1 teaspoon sugar
½ teaspoon ground cinnamon
1½ teaspoons apple cider vinegar
¼ teaspoon ground cumin
⅛ teaspoon cayenne pepper

For Serving

4 (6-inch) hero rolls, tops split like a hotdog bun
¾ cup Chimichurri (page 227)

1 **MAKE THE CHORIZO PATTIES:** In a large bowl, use your clean hands to combine the pork, garlic, tomato paste, paprikas, salt, sugar, cinnamon, vinegar, cumin, and cayenne. Use your hands to form four equal-size patties.

2 Heat a wide cast-iron skillet or carbon-steel skillet over medium heat. Place the chorizo patties in the pan, pressing each one gently into the pan for about 10 seconds to create good contact. Sear for 2 minutes, then flip all the patties and cook for 2 minutes. Flip once more and cook for a final minute. Remove from the heat.

3 Chop each chorizo patty into thirds so that it will fill the length of the roll. Place the chorizo on the rolls, top each sandwich with 3 tablespoons of the chimichurri, and serve.

Sweet & Smoky Ribs

Serves 4 to 6

Barbecue is one of America's greatest culinary genres. Of course, many cultures have cooked in a similar style throughout history—overnight, underground, or with woodsmoke. But there's something special about our pit cooking, smoking, dry rubs, vinegars, and regional variations. American barbecue is its own thing, even if it stands on the shoulders of giants. Ribs are a staple, and they happen to be an easy foot into the world of BBQ. Mine are made with a sweet and sticky pineapple sauce—a nod to pineapple and bacon on pizza (which is delicious), and to tacos al pastor, my favorite taco preparation.

For the Baby Back Ribs

2 (3-pound) racks baby back ribs
2 teaspoons kosher salt
2 teaspoons granulated garlic
2 teaspoons smoked paprika
1½ teaspoons chili powder
1 teaspoon freshly ground black pepper

For the Pineapple BBQ Sauce

1 cup ketchup
½ cup molasses
½ cup canned crushed pineapple
¼ cup apple cider vinegar
¼ cup chopped canned chipotle peppers in adobo sauce
3 tablespoons Worcestershire sauce
1 teaspoon granulated garlic
1 teaspoon hot paprika
1 teaspoon yellow mustard
½ teaspoon kosher salt
½ teaspoon freshly ground black pepper

1 **MAKE THE RIBS:** Preheat the oven to 275°F. Line a baking sheet (or two, if needed) with aluminum foil.

2 Place the ribs meat-side down on the prepared baking sheet. Run a paring knife down the middle, perpendicular to the bones, for the length of the rack, releasing the thin membrane. Make a small tab you can grab by creating another incision in the membrane. Then, using paper towel to help you grip, pull off and discard the membrane.

3 In a small bowl, whisk together the salt, granulated garlic, smoked paprika, chili powder, and black pepper. Season the ribs all over with the spice rub, gently rubbing it in. Place the ribs meat-side up and tightly cover the baking sheet with foil. Bake for 2 to 2½ hours, until the meat begins to pull away from the ends of the bones and the ribs are very flexible and soft.

4 **MEANWHILE, MAKE THE BBQ SAUCE:** In a small saucepan, combine the ketchup, molasses, pineapple, vinegar, chipotles, Worcestershire, granulated garlic, hot paprika, mustard, salt, and black pepper. Bring to a boil over high heat, then reduce the heat to medium and cook until reduced by a third, about 10 minutes. Remove from the heat and let the sauce cool to room temperature, then refrigerate until ready to use (it will keep for up to 1 week).

5 Remove the ribs from the oven and discard the foil. Drain any excess liquid from the baking sheet. Increase the oven temperature to 425°F. Brush two-thirds of the BBQ sauce onto the tops of the ribs and return them to the oven. Bake for 20 to 25 minutes more, until the sauce has caramelized and the ribs are very tender.

6 Remove from the oven and let cool for 15 minutes, then transfer to a cutting board. Cut in between each rib and serve with the remaining BBQ sauce alongside for dousing and dipping.

POULTRY & PORK

Whole Chicken

WITH BRIGHT SPICES, LEMON & POTATOES

Serves 2 to 4

Marcella Hazan, the world-famous Italian cookbook author, made the best whole roasted chicken. It's as simple as salt and a lemon poked with several holes, yet it's a masterpiece. I've built on her lemony goodness with spices that accentuate the fruit's acidity, and I cook the chicken over potatoes, which catch the drippings and become a hearty side. It's a complete meal, and it couldn't exist without Marcella. True story: My grandfather Frank used to work with Marcella and her husband, Victor. As a result of that decades-long relationship, I was able to spend an afternoon with her. Marcella Hazan cooked me lunch once—it was epic.

1½ pounds small red potatoes, halved if large
2½ tablespoons extra-virgin olive oil
2 teaspoons kosher salt
1½ teaspoons ground cumin
1 teaspoon ground coriander
½ teaspoon freshly ground black pepper
1 large lemon
1 (4-pound) whole chicken
1 head garlic, halved crosswise

1 Position a rack in the lower third of the oven and preheat to 425°F.

2 Place the potatoes in the bottom of a roasting pan. Drizzle with 2 tablespoons of the olive oil and season with ½ teaspoon of the salt.

3 In a small bowl, combine the cumin, coriander, 1¼ teaspoons of the salt, and the pepper. Using a wooden skewer, toothpick, or the tip of a paring knife, puncture the lemon all over its surface.

4 Fit a wire rack inside the roasting pan, over the potatoes, and place the chicken on top, breast-side up. Season the cavity of the chicken with the remaining ¼ teaspoon salt, then add one half of the garlic head, the punctured lemon, and the other half of the garlic. Rub or brush the remaining ½ tablespoon olive oil all over the outside of the bird; this is mostly to create a "glue" for the spices to stick to. Evenly sprinkle on the spice mixture.

5 Roast the chicken for about 1 hour, until an instant-read thermometer inserted into the thickest part of the thigh reads 160°F. Remove from the oven and let rest for 15 to 20 minutes. Carve the chicken and serve it alongside the potatoes.

Rosemary Brick Chicken

Serves 2 to 4

Personally, I hate the phrase "it tastes like chicken," as the assumption is that you're describing something palatable, bland, and easy for anyone to eat—something that tastes like nothing! This recipe is worlds away from that overused catchphrase. Thigh meat is juicy and flavorful, and cooking it over high heat with something heavy on top to weight it down against the pan increases the browning of the meat and makes for more even cooking. Crank that hood vent and crack a window—let's make everyone say, "I've never had chicken that tastes like this!"

4 to 6 boneless, skinless chicken thighs
¼ cup plain full-fat Greek yogurt
2 tablespoons extra-virgin olive oil
1½ teaspoons kosher salt
1 teaspoon freshly ground black pepper
1½ tablespoons fresh rosemary leaves
Zest of 1 lemon

For Serving

Chimichurri, homemade (page 227) or store-bought
Red Pepper Olive Oil (page 226), or extra-virgin olive oil and red pepper flakes
Flaky salt

1 In a 9 × 13-inch baking dish, combine the chicken, yogurt, olive oil, salt, pepper, rosemary, and lemon zest. Rub the marinade into every crevice. Let the chicken marinate at room temperature for at least 15 minutes or up to 1 hour, or cover with plastic wrap and let marinate in the refrigerator overnight.

2 Cover the cooking surface of a large cast-iron skillet with parchment paper and heat the pan over medium-high heat. When it just begins to smoke, working in batches as needed, place the chicken cut-side up on the parchment. Place a large brick wrapped in aluminum foil or a second heavy skillet directly on top of the chicken. Cook until the chicken has flattened and has a nice dark brown crust on the bottom, 4 to 5 minutes. Remove the brick or skillet, flip the chicken, and cook until cooked through, 1 minute more. Remove from the heat and let the chicken rest in the pan for 2 minutes; an instant-read thermometer inserted into the thickest part of the thigh should read at least 165°F.

3 Serve dolloped with chimichurri, drizzled with red pepper olive oil, and sprinkled with flaky salt.

New York Street Cart-Style Chicken & Rice

Serves 4

When you're in New York City, no meal is more flavorful and consistently good than chicken and rice from the corner cart. Each vendor has their own spice blends for the meats, making each tray its own special experience. They're often open into the wee hours of the morning—when I visit one, I like to chat with the vendor about their day, and often that camaraderie yields a few pieces of fried eggplant, or a 50/50 blend of lamb and chicken, and an extra squeeze of both the hot sauce and the white sauce. Since I no longer live in the City that Never Sleeps, I had to make my own version, and this one hits the spot.

For the Rice

2 cups long-grain white rice
2 tablespoons unsalted butter
1 tablespoon ground turmeric
1 teaspoon sweet paprika
½ teaspoon kosher salt
½ teaspoon granulated garlic

For the White Sauce

½ cup plain nonfat Greek yogurt
2 tablespoons mayonnaise
2 tablespoons fresh lemon juice
1 teaspoon grated garlic
¼ teaspoon sugar
⅛ teaspoon kosher salt

For the Chicken

4 to 6 boneless, skinless chicken thighs
¼ cup distilled white vinegar
1 tablespoon smoked paprika
1 teaspoon granulated garlic
1 teaspoon dried oregano
1 teaspoon ground cumin
1 teaspoon sugar
1½ teaspoons kosher salt
½ teaspoon freshly ground black pepper
¼ teaspoon cayenne pepper
2 tablespoons neutral oil

For Serving

Shredded lettuce
Diced tomato
Hot sauce

1 **MAKE THE RICE:** Place the rice in a medium bowl and add water to cover by 2 inches. Let soak for 10 minutes, then drain and rinse.

2 In a medium saucepan, combine 2 cups water, the butter, turmeric, paprika, salt, and granulated garlic. Add the rice and bring to a simmer over high heat, then cover and reduce the heat to low. Cook for 15 minutes, then remove from the heat and let stand, still covered, for 5 minutes more. Remove the lid and fluff the rice with a fork.

3 **MEANWHILE, MAKE THE WHITE SAUCE:** In a small bowl, stir together the yogurt, mayonnaise, lemon juice, garlic, sugar, and salt until smooth.

4 **MAKE THE CHICKEN:** Cut the chicken thighs into 1- to 2-inch pieces and place them in a medium bowl. Add the vinegar, smoked paprika, granulated garlic, oregano, cumin, sugar, salt, black pepper, and cayenne. Toss to coat and let marinate at room temperature for at least 15 minutes or up to 1 hour, or cover with plastic wrap and let marinate in the refrigerator overnight.

5 In a large skillet, heat the oil over medium-high heat. When the oil is shimmering, add the chicken and cook, stirring occasionally, until the pieces are firm and cooked through, about 10 minutes.

6 To serve it like the street vendors, on plates, create a row of rice, a row of chicken, and a row of lettuce and tomato, if using. Top it all with white sauce and add hot sauce to taste.

Pork Cutlet

WITH FENNEL SLAW

Serves 4

Few dishes are as perfect as wiener schnitzel, a thinly pounded veal chop that's deep-fried until golden and served with lemon wedges for squeezing over the top. I grew up with breaded chicken cutlets, but the first time I tasted the original real-deal schnitzel in Europe, my world changed. It was familiar but different, simple but perfect. This pork cutlet is inspired by that jewel of a recipe, and it's a good one! The perfectly salty, golden, crispy breading reminds me that making cutlets of any kind is always worth the time, especially if balanced by a punchy dressing and crunchy slaw!

- 2 large fennel bulbs, thinly sliced
- 2 pears, thinly sliced
- ⅓ cup Punchy Vinaigrette (page 225) or store-bought vinaigrette
- 1½ teaspoons kosher salt
- 1¼ teaspoons freshly ground black pepper
- 1½ cups panko breadcrumbs
- 1 cup all-purpose flour
- 2 large eggs
- 1 ounce club soda or sparkling water
- 4 (6-ounce) boneless pork chops
- ¾ cup neutral oil, plus more if needed
- Flaky salt (optional)
- Lemon wedges, for serving

1 In a large bowl, combine the fennel, pears, vinaigrette, ½ teaspoon of the salt, and ¼ teaspoon of the pepper. Toss to coat well.

2 In a high-powered blender or food processor, blend the panko on high speed speed until you have an ultrafine powder. Transfer to a shallow bowl. In a second shallow bowl, place the flour. In a third, whisk together the eggs and the club soda.

3 On a plastic cutting board or large piece of plastic wrap, lay the pork chops out flat. Working with one at a time, place your nondominant hand on top of a pork chop, then use a sharp knife to slice it in half horizontally, leaving the last bit intact as a hinge so you can open the chop like a book. Use a meat pounder or small, heavy skillet to pound the butterflied chops to a ½-inch thickness.

4 In a large skillet, heat ½ cup of the oil over medium-high heat. Season the cutlets all over with ⅛ teaspoon each of the salt and pepper on each side. Working with two at a time, add the cutlets to the flour, pressing to adhere. Then dip them in the egg mixture, turning to coat well and allowing any excess to drip off. Transfer them to the breadcrumbs, pressing to adhere.

5 When the oil is shimmering, gently drop the breaded cutlets into the skillet. Vigorously shake the pan back and forth to force some of the oil over the tops of the cutlets. Cook until deeply golden brown on the bottom, 3 to 4 minutes, then flip and cook until the second side is browned, 2 minutes more. Transfer to a paper towel–lined plate. Repeat with the remaining cutlets, adding more oil to the skillet as needed between batches and heating it until shimmering before adding the cutlets.

6 Finish the cutlets with flaky salt, if desired. Serve with the fennel and pear slaw alongside and lemon wedges for squeezing.

Curry Chicken Potpie

Serves 2 to 4

If you look at rotisserie chicken as an ingredient, you can speed up the tasks involved in getting all kinds of chicken dishes onto the table. My potpie is one example that uses this particular shortcut. The filling leans into the flavors of a slightly spiced chicken salad, and is topped with a sheet of puff pastry before being baked until golden and flaky. Upon taking a bite, food photographer Lauren Volo said it best: "This is way more delicious than it has any right to be." I concur—it seems too easy for how good it tastes!

- 1 tablespoon extra-virgin olive oil
- 2 carrots, diced
- 1 large shallot, diced
- 1 teaspoon bouillon paste, such as Better Than Bouillon
- 2 teaspoons curry powder
- 1 (13.5-ounce) can coconut cream
- ⅛ teaspoon kosher salt
- ¼ teaspoon freshly ground black pepper
- 1 (1¾-pound) rotisserie chicken, meat shredded and skin coarsely chopped (about 2 cups)
- 1 tablespoon cornstarch
- 1 sheet frozen puff pastry (from a 17-ounce box), thawed
- 1 large egg, beaten

1 Preheat the oven to 425°F.

2 In a 10-inch cast-iron skillet, combine the olive oil, carrots, and shallot over medium heat. Cook, stirring, until the shallots are just beginning to soften, about 3 minutes. Add the bouillon and curry powder and cook, stirring, until the spices are fragrant and the shallots and carrots have softened, 6 to 8 minutes; if the spices begin to burn, add 2 tablespoons water to the skillet. Stir in the coconut cream, salt, pepper, and shredded chicken and chopped skin. Bring to a light simmer, then remove from the heat.

3 In a small bowl, whisk together the cornstarch and 2 tablespoons water until smooth. Stir the mixture into the skillet.

4 Unroll the puff pastry on top of the chicken mixture and trim any overhanging pastry to 1 inch. (If the pastry doesn't fully cover the mixture, that's okay, as long as it's covering 75 percent; if not, roll it out on the counter until it's wide enough.) Use a knife tip to make five 2-inch-long slits in the pastry. Brush the pastry with the egg.

5 Place the skillet on a baking sheet and bake for 20 to 25 minutes, until the pastry is deep golden. Remove from the oven and let cool for 10 minutes before serving.

Sheet Pan Pork Chops

WITH APPLE & SWISS CHARD

Serves 4

Pork chops and apple have long been a winning combination. The flavors are complementary: salty, porky, juicy meat with sweet, warming, delicate roasted apples. In the fall and winter, chops and apples are one of my go-to dishes for hearty nourishment. To simplify the cooking process, these chops are seared hard on one side only for color and flavor, then cooked through (pretty quickly) alongside the apples on a baking sheet. Because pork chops are lean, keeping them juicy and perfectly cooked is paramount. A thermometer will ensure the desired outcome.

- 2 Honeycrisp apples, cut into wedges
- 3 tablespoons extra-virgin olive oil
- 1½ teaspoons kosher salt
- 4 (12-ounce) bone-in pork chops
- 1 bunch Swiss chard, leaves stemmed and cut into 1-inch-wide strips
- ½ teaspoon freshly ground black pepper
- ¼ cup stone-ground mustard
- 1 tablespoon apple cider vinegar
- 1 garlic clove, grated
- 1 tablespoon honey
- 1 tablespoon mayonnaise

1 Preheat the oven to 425°F. Line a baking sheet with aluminum foil.

2 On the prepared baking sheet, toss the apples with 1 tablespoon of the olive oil and ¼ teaspoon of the salt. Bake for about 15 minutes, until the apples have begun to caramelize around the edges and soften in the middle.

3 Meanwhile, season the pork chops with ⅛ teaspoon of the salt on each side. Heat a large skillet over medium-high heat, then pour in 1 tablespoon of the olive oil. When the oil is shimmering, working in batches as needed, add the pork chops and cook until deeply golden brown on the bottom, 4 to 6 minutes. Transfer to a plate, seared-side up.

4 Remove the baking sheet from the oven and push the apples onto one-third of the baking sheet. Add the pork chops, seared-side up, on the middle third, followed by the Swiss chard on the final third of the pan (it will be piled high). Season the chard with the remaining 1 tablespoon olive oil, remaining ¼ teaspoon salt, and ¼ teaspoon of the pepper.

5 Return the baking sheet to the oven and bake until an instant-read thermometer inserted into the thickest part of the pork chops reaches 145°F, and the Swiss chard is wilted, 10 to 15 minutes. Remove from the oven and let the pork rest for about 5 minutes.

6 Meanwhile, in a small bowl, whisk together the mustard, vinegar, garlic, honey, mayonnaise, and remaining ¼ teaspoon pepper.

7 Divide the pork, apples, and chard among plates and serve with the mustard sauce spooned over the top.

SABRE
PARIS

Duck Salad

Serves 2 as a main or 4 as a starter

"I'm a sucker for duck." These were the words spoken by my friend Trent's dad after an evening special was presented to him at a restaurant. It always stuck in my head, because you know what? I'm a sucker for duck, too. I grew up with Peking duck from Shun Lee and have grown to love many preparations since then. Duck breasts are super fatty; the key to deliciousness is to slowly cook out that fat to melt it. That richness is paired and balanced out with this beautiful salad that's all the work of the humble vegetable peeler. I think you've got a new classic on your hands.

For the Dressing

¼ cup fish sauce
Zest and juice of 1 lime
2 tablespoons dark brown sugar
2 garlic cloves, grated
2 Thai bird's-eye chilies, finely chopped, or 1 teaspoon Sweet & Zingy Fresno Chilies (page 230) or red pepper flakes

For the Duck

2 (8-ounce) duck breasts
1 teaspoon kosher salt

For the Salad

½ English cucumber, peeled, shaved into long ribbons with a vegetable peeler
½ small daikon radish, peeled, shaved into long ribbons with a vegetable peeler
2 carrots, peeled, shaved into long ribbons with a vegetable peeler
1 cup cherry tomatoes, halved
1 cup fresh cilantro leaves
1 cup fresh mint leaves

1 **MAKE THE DRESSING:** In a small bowl, whisk together the fish sauce, lime zest and juice, brown sugar, garlic, and chilies until the sugar is dissolved.

2 **MAKE THE DUCK:** Pat the duck breasts completely dry, then score the fatty side into a very tight crosshatch pattern. Use almost no pressure when scoring, being sure to only cut the skin and avoid the flesh. Season the fatty sides with ¾ teaspoon of the salt.

3 Place the duck breasts, fatty sides down, in a large heavy-bottomed skillet. Adjust the heat between medium-low and low, listening carefully: Cooking should be silent for the first 5 minutes; if it's sputtering or sizzling, reduce the heat. After 5 minutes, increase the heat if needed to create a gentle, consistent popping rhythm. Cook until the skin is golden brown and an instant-read thermometer inserted into the flesh reads 125°F, about 10 minutes more. Season the flesh sides with the remaining ¼ teaspoon salt, then flip and cook until the flesh side is no longer raw, 1 to 2 minutes for medium rare. Transfer the duck to a wire rack and let it rest for 5 to 10 minutes.

4 **MEANWHILE, MAKE THE SALAD:** In a large bowl, combine the cucumber, radish, carrots, cherry tomatoes, cilantro, and mint. Reserve 2 tablespoons of the dressing, then pour the remainder into the bowl with the vegetables. Gently toss to coat. Let the salad marinate for 5 to 10 minutes, tossing again halfway through.

5 Cut the duck breasts into ½-inch-thick slices. Arrange the salad on a serving platter and top with the duck. Drizzle the reserved dressing over the top and serve immediately.

Fried Chicken Sandwich

Makes 4 sandwiches

For about two years, new fried chicken sandwich spots were popping up all over New York, and it seemed like the cheeseburger's crown might be challenged. That didn't happen, but it did open my eyes to the endless possibilities of fried chicken sandwiches as I tried the offerings from Blue Ribbon, Pies 'n Thighs, and Win Son, among others. As I ate my way through this "research," I started imagining my dream sandwich. I like dark meat—it stays extra juicy when fried and it's much more forgiving. I love the Taiwanese style of breading chicken with cornstarch or potato starch, which yields an extra-crispy coating. And I love a sweet pickle brine. Combine those elements and you have absolute perfection.

½ cup spicy pickle brine, or ½ cup pickle brine plus 1 teaspoon cayenne pepper
1 tablespoon smoked paprika
1 teaspoon kosher salt, plus more for serving
½ teaspoon granulated garlic
½ teaspoon cayenne pepper
½ teaspoon freshly ground black pepper
4 boneless, skinless chicken thighs
½ cup potato starch
½ cup all-purpose flour
4 to 8 cups neutral oil, for frying

For Serving

4 potato rolls, split
Bread-and-butter pickles or Sweet & Zingy Fresno Chilies (page 230)
Mayonnaise

1 In a medium bowl, stir together the pickle brine, paprika, salt, granulated garlic, cayenne, and black pepper. Add the chicken, turn to coat, and set aside to marinate at room temperature for at least 15 minutes or up to 1 hour, or cover with plastic wrap and refrigerate overnight.

2 In a separate bowl, whisk together the potato starch and flour.

3 Line a baking sheet with parchment paper, then set a wire rack on top. Fill a large Dutch oven halfway with oil. Clip a deep-fry thermometer to the side of the pot and heat over medium-high heat to 325°F. When the oil is at temperature, add 1 tablespoon of the marinade to the flour mixture and mix well with a fork; it should form some lumpy bits. Add 2 chicken thighs to the flour mixture and turn to coat, pressing the flour mixture to adhere. Drop the chicken into the oil and cook for exactly 2 minutes, then transfer the chicken to the prepared rack. Repeat with the remaining chicken.

4 Bring the oil back to 325°F. Return the first batch of chicken to the oil and cook for 5 minutes, flipping halfway through. Transfer the chicken to the rack; an instant-read thermometer inserted into the deepest point should be at least 165°F. Season each piece immediately with a light sprinkling of salt. Repeat with the remaining chicken.

5 To assemble the sandwiches, layer pickles onto the bottom buns and slather mayonnaise inside the top buns. Place the chicken in the middle and enjoy!

NOTE: When deep-frying, your utensils must be completely dry to prevent the hot oil from sputtering violently, which can be dangerous.

Paprika Chicken

Serves 4 to 6

There's a humongous group of home chefs who share recipes in the *Struggle Meals* Facebook group. I pop in often, usually to get some inspiration from what I consider to be a hive mind of savvy, like-minded cooks. Posting "What should I make, what do you want to see from me?" yielded numerous calls for chicken paprikash, a Hungarian stew. As you might guess, paprika is a huge element in this dish, and sweet Hungarian paprika specifically is the way to go here; using all smoked paprika will result in an acrid, ash-like undertone. My version is skinless, boneless, and an absolute winner for dinner.

For the Chicken

- 4 to 6 boneless, skinless chicken thighs
- 1 teaspoon kosher salt
- ¼ teaspoon freshly ground black pepper
- 2 tablespoons neutral oil
- 1 tablespoon extra-virgin olive oil
- 2 medium yellow onions, diced
- 1 tablespoon tomato paste
- ¼ cup sweet paprika
- 1 teaspoon smoked paprika, hot paprika, or cayenne pepper
- ¼ cup dry white wine
- 1 cup low-sodium chicken broth

For the Rice

- 2 cups long-grain white rice or basmati rice
- 2 tablespoons unsalted butter
- ½ teaspoon kosher salt
- ½ cup chopped fresh parsley

1 MAKE THE CHICKEN: Heat a large skillet over medium-high heat. Pat the chicken dry, then season it on both sides with ½ teaspoon of the salt and the pepper. Pour the neutral oil into the pan; it should shimmer immediately. Working in batches as needed, add the chicken and cook until browned on the outside but not quite cooked through, about 5 minutes per side. Transfer the chicken to a plate.

2 Reduce the heat to medium and add the olive oil, onions, and the remaining ½ teaspoon salt. Cook, stirring occasionally, until the onions are translucent and just beginning to brown, 6 to 8 minutes. Add the tomato paste and paprikas and cook, stirring, until the paste darkens and the spices are fragrant, about 1 minute.

3 Pour in the wine and cook until the alcohol evaporates, about 1 minute. Add the broth and bring to a simmer, increasing the heat as needed. Return the chicken to the pan, along with any collected juices. Reduce the heat to low, cover, and cook for 20 minutes, then remove the lid and simmer until the sauce is slightly thickened, about 5 minutes more.

4 MEANWHILE, MAKE THE RICE: Place the rice in a medium bowl and add water to cover by 2 inches. Let soak for 10 minutes, then drain and rinse.

5 In a medium saucepan, combine 2 cups water, the butter, and salt.

6 Add the rice and bring to a simmer over high heat, then then cover and reduce the heat to low. Cook for 15 minutes, then remove from the heat and let stand, still covered, for 5 minutes more.

7 Remove the lid, add the parsley, and fluff the rice with a fork. Serve immediately or cover to keep warm until the chicken is ready.

8 Divide the rice among bowls, top with the chicken and sauce, and serve.

Garlic Turkey Meatloaf

Serves 4

I love Bolognese, I love hamburgers, I love meatballs, but it is my personal opinion that beef in meatloaf is overkill. Blasphemous, I know. But turkey is leaner and cleaner, and pairs better with the classic sweet and sticky elements of meatloaf, allowing more room for other ingredients to shine. Fresh garlic, parsley, and mustard all punch through in a turkey meatloaf, yielding a more, dare I say, sophisticated flavor profile.

For the Glaze

½ cup ketchup
1 tablespoon Dijon mustard
2 tablespoons dark brown sugar
1 tablespoon Worcestershire sauce

For the Meatloaf

1 tablespoon unsalted butter
1 small yellow onion, diced
1¾ teaspoons kosher salt
10 garlic cloves, thinly sliced
½ cup plain breadcrumbs
2 large eggs
1 small bunch parsley, finely chopped
½ teaspoon freshly ground black pepper
2 pounds 93% lean ground turkey

1 Position a rack in the center of the oven and preheat to 350°F. Line a baking sheet with aluminum foil.

2 **MAKE THE GLAZE:** In a small bowl, whisk together the ketchup, Dijon mustard, brown sugar, and Worcestershire sauce. Set aside.

3 **MAKE THE MEATLOAF:** In a small skillet over medium heat, combine the butter, onion, and ¼ teaspoon of the salt. Cook until the onions have released some of their liquid, 2 to 3 minutes, then add the garlic. Cook, stirring occasionally, until the garlic has softened and the onions are translucent, 4 to 5 minutes. Transfer to a large bowl to let cool slightly.

4 Add the breadcrumbs, eggs, parsley, remaining 1½ teaspoons salt, the pepper, and ¼ cup of the glaze to the onion mixture and whisk to combine. Let the breadcrumbs soften for 2 to 3 minutes, then add the ground turkey. Use your hands to gently combine. Transfer the meat mixture to the prepared baking sheet and form into a 9 × 6-inch loaf. Brush the remaining glaze evenly over the top and sides.

5 Bake the meatloaf for about 45 minutes, until an instant-read thermometer inserted into the center reads 160°F, then turn the oven to broil and cook for 2 to 5 minutes, until the glaze thickens and turns brown in a few spots. Remove the meatloaf from the oven and let rest for about 5 minutes so it stays together and retains its juices when sliced. Cut into thick slices and enjoy.

FISH & SEAFOOD

Grilled Calamari Salad

Serves 4 as a starter

If you've only ever tried fried calamari, you're missing out. Grilled fresh calamari has a great texture and tastes delicious hot or cold. In this recipe, tubes are cooked whole then sliced after. The broiler is my choice for cooking here, as it's easy, consistent, and hot, but keeping the tubes whole also allows the option of grilling outside over charcoal, if you have such a setup. The lemon dressing allows this meaty salad to defy gravity with lightness and brightness.

2 pounds calamari tubes, poked a few times with the tip of a skewer for drainage
3 tablespoons neutral oil or extra-virgin olive oil
1 tablespoon sweet paprika
½ teaspoon kosher salt
¼ teaspoon freshly ground black pepper
2 tablespoons lemon dressing, homemade (page 225) or store-bought
¼ cup chopped sun-dried tomatoes
Flaky salt
1 lemon, for squeezing and serving

1 Position an oven rack 6 to 8 inches from the broiler heat source and preheat the broiler. Line a baking sheet with aluminum foil and set a wire rack on top.

2 In a medium bowl, combine the calamari, oil, paprika, salt, and pepper. Toss to coat well. Arrange the calamari on the prepared rack, spacing them apart, and broil for 2 minutes, until the edges are just beginning to brown and they've curled up slightly. Flip each calamari and broil for 2 to 3 minutes more, until the paprika is just beginning to brown. Remove the calamari from the oven and let cool for about 5 minutes, then slice each tube into ½-inch-thick rings.

3 Transfer the calamari to a medium bowl. Add the lemon dressing and the sun-dried tomatoes and toss to combine. Finish with flaky salt and fresh lemon juice before serving family-style.

Miso Salmon & Chive Rice

Serves 4

For ten years, one of my favorite affordable dinners was from Mooncake Foods, a now defunct takeout spot (with tables) at the mouth of the Holland Tunnel. I'd sit at the bar and eat my $10 miso salmon with Chinese broccoli and brown rice while the folks heading to New Jersey laid into their car horns through entire traffic light cycles. The restaurant might have closed, but that dish never left me: It was sweet, meaty, slightly brûléed, always filling, and always quickly made. My dish is inspired by theirs, and it brings back great memories (but thankfully none of loud honking).

For the Rice

- 1½ cups medium-grain white rice
- 1 tablespoon sesame seeds
- 1 tablespoon chopped fresh chives

For the Fish

- ¼ cup white miso paste
- 2 tablespoons apple cider vinegar
- 2 tablespoons pure maple syrup
- 2 teaspoons sugar
- 1 teaspoon low-sodium soy sauce
- 4 (6-ounce) salmon fillets

1 **MAKE THE RICE:** Rinse the rice in a fine-mesh sieve under cool running water, moving it around with your hand until the water runs clear. Transfer the rice to a medium pot, add 1½ cups water, and let the rice soak for 10 minutes.

2 Bring the water to a simmer over medium heat, then reduce the heat to low, cover, and steam for 20 minutes. Remove from the heat and let stand, still covered, for 10 minutes. Fluff the rice well with a fork, and either serve immediately or return the lid to the pot and hold the rice until the fish is ready.

3 **MEANWHILE, MAKE THE FISH:** In a 9-inch square baking dish, whisk together the miso, cider vinegar, maple syrup, sugar, and soy sauce. Add the salmon, skin-side up. Cover tightly and set aside to marinate at room temperature for at least 45 minutes, or in the refrigerator overnight.

4 Position a rack in the center of the oven and preheat to 425°F. Line a baking sheet with aluminum foil.

5 Remove the salmon from the marinade, allowing the excess to drip off. Place the fish skin-side down on the prepared baking sheet. Lightly brush a little more marinade onto each fillet to aid in the brûlée.

6 Roast the fish for about 10 minutes, then turn on the broiler and cook the salmon for 2 to 4 minutes more, until charred in most spots and the edges are browned. Remove from the oven and let rest for about 2 minutes before serving.

7 Divide the fish among plates and serve the rice topped with the sesame seeds and the chives.

Shrimp with Spicy Garlic Butter

Serves 4

I've always thought of shrimp as tiny lobsters, and I can only think of lobster being doused in butter. Does this make sense? I'm not sure, but shrimp are pretty mild and very lean—it's no wonder butter is a great choice. Even better if that butter is spicy and garlicky! Here's a one-pot, easy-to-make flavor bomb of your shrimp dreams. Eat it hot—on its own with crusty bread, or as the filling to a po'boy sandwich.

6 tablespoons (¾ stick) unsalted butter, at room temperature
6 garlic cloves, minced
1 tablespoon Calabrian chili paste
1 pound large shrimp, peeled and deveined
1 teaspoon kosher salt
½ teaspoon freshly ground black pepper
¼ cup dry white wine
1 tablespoon sherry vinegar
2 tablespoons chopped fresh parsley
1 baguette, cut into 8 slices and toasted

1 In a small bowl, stir together the butter, garlic, and Calabrian chili paste. Transfer the butter mixture to a 12-inch skillet and heat over medium heat. Add the shrimp and season with ½ teaspoon of the salt and the pepper. Cook, undisturbed, until the shrimp turn pink on the bottom, about 2 minutes. Flip the shrimp, season with the remaining ½ teaspoon salt, and cook until the shrimp are pink, opaque, and beginning to curl, 2 minutes more.

2 Reduce the heat to low. Pour in the wine and the vinegar. Swirl the pan and cook until the sauce thickens slightly but is still brothy, about 1 minute.

3 Divide the shrimp and sauce among shallow bowls. Sprinkle with parsley and serve with the toasted baguette alongside for dipping.

Roasted Branzino

WITH CILANTRO SALAD

Serves 4

Once you've made a few fish fillet dishes, you're ready to graduate to a whole roasted fish. Branzino is a mild, clean-tasting fish that you can easily serve whole to each person. For this recipe, I stuff the fish with garlic and ginger, flavors I love from Malaysian-style steamed fish. As these aromatics steam inside the roasting fish, it smells incredible, and so I push the flavors even more with cilantro—not as a garnish, but as a full-on dressed herb salad.

For the Roasted Branzino

- 4 (1- to 1½-pound) whole branzini, scaled and gutted
- 3 tablespoons extra-virgin olive oil
- 3 teaspoons kosher salt
- 4 scallions, cut into 2-inch pieces
- 6 garlic cloves, sliced
- 1 (2-inch) piece fresh ginger, peeled and sliced

For the Cilantro Salad

- 2 tablespoons low-sodium soy sauce
- 2 tablespoons fresh lime juice
- 1 tablespoon chili crisp
- 1 teaspoon toasted sesame oil
- ½ teaspoon sugar
- 1 large bunch cilantro
- 2 scallions, thinly sliced

1 Position a rack in the upper third of the oven and preheat to 450°F. Line a baking sheet with aluminum foil.

2 **MAKE THE BRANZINO:** Place the fish on the prepared baking sheet and drizzle the olive oil evenly over them. Rub the oil all over both sides of each fish.

3 Season the inside of each fish with ¼ teaspoon of the salt per fish, then stuff them with the scallions, garlic, and ginger, dividing them evenly. Close the fish so they lay on their sides. Season the outside of the fish with the remaining 2 teaspoons salt, dividing it evenly among them.

4 Roast the fish for 15 to 18 minutes, until the skin begins to tighten and very slightly darken and the fish feels mostly firm to the touch in its thickest part. Turn the oven to broil and cook the fish for 1 to 3 minutes more, until the spots with the deepest browning are just shy of burning. Remove the fish from the oven and let cool slightly.

5 **MEANWHILE, MAKE THE SALAD:** In a medium bowl, whisk together the soy sauce, lime juice, chili crisp, sesame oil, and the sugar until the sugar is fully dissolved. Add the cilantro and the scallions and gently toss to combine.

6 Divide the fish among four plates and serve with some salad on the side—watch for small bones as you enjoy!

Spicy Poached Cod

Serves 4

My true, conscious, culinary journey began on a small boat in Italy. Not only did I deeply connect with the improvisational cooking of my uncle Andrea, but I also understood that simplicity is often best. *Pesce all'aqua pazza* translates to "fish in crazy water." Crazy water, of course, can be any liquid—as long as it's flavorful. Uncle Andrea would dip a bucket over the edge of the boat and fill it with salty Tyrrhenian seawater. Back in the kitchen, he'd add capers, Calabrian chili peppers, fresh oregano, tomatoes that had been sitting in the sun all day, and sometimes even olives. Whatever we caught that day was then poached, boiled, and steamed all at once in just minutes. It was a revelation! Fish, often viewed as fussy and hard to make at home, was simplified with this "crazy" blueprint. My version uses cod, and the aqua pazza is a combination of white wine, tomatoes, jalapeños, salt, parsley, and Calabrian chili peppers. You'd be crazy *not* to try it. And make sure to mop up all the crazy water with the fried bread, an act known as *fare la scarpetta* at Italian dinner tables.

- 4 tablespoons extra-virgin olive oil
- 4 slices sourdough bread or ciabatta
- 4 garlic cloves, sliced
- 1 jalapeño, sliced
- 4 (6-ounce) cod fillets
- 1 pint cherry tomatoes, halved
- ¼ cup dry white wine
- ⅓ cup chopped fresh parsley
- 1½ teaspoons kosher salt, plus more as needed
- 2 teaspoons Calabrian chili paste

1 In a medium skillet, heat 1 tablespoon of the olive oil over medium heat. When the oil is shimmering, add 2 slices of the bread. Cook until golden brown on both sides side, about 3 minutes total, then transfer to a plate. Repeat with another 1 tablespoon olive oil and the remaining 2 slices bread.

2 In the same skillet (no need to wipe it out), combine the remaining 2 tablespoons olive oil, the garlic, and jalapeño. Cook, stirring, until the garlic begins to char slightly around the edges, about 2 minutes. Spread the garlic and jalapeños in an even layer in the bottom of the pan and place the cod on top, spacing the fillets apart.

3 Add ½ cup water, the cherry tomatoes, wine, and parsley. Increase the heat and bring to a simmer, then reduce the heat to low. Sprinkle the salt over the fish, dividing evenly, then cover the pan and cook until the cod flakes apart when prodded with a fork, about 5 minutes. Transfer each fillet to a shallow individual serving bowl.

4 Increase the heat under the pot to high and bring the broth to a boil. Add the Calabrian chili paste and cook, stirring vigorously, until the liquid has reduced by one-quarter, about 2 minutes. Taste the broth and adjust the seasoning as needed.

5 Spoon the broth over the fillets, dividing it evenly, and serve with the fried bread alongside for dipping.

Crispy Arctic Char

WITH SPICY BROWN BUTTER TOMATOES

Serves 4

The flesh of arctic char looks a lot like that of salmon, and the two fish even taste somewhat similar, but their skin is completely different. Char is a scaleless fish like trout, and the skin becomes shatteringly crisp when seared. You don't want to miss out on this treat! Use a piece of parchment directly in your skillet to create a nonstick surface, and let 'er rip—gently. The brown butter tomatoes are easy to make while the fish cooks and add a nice counterpoint to this rich and exciting preparation.

For the Brown Butter Tomatoes

1 pint cherry tomatoes
6 pickled banana pepper slices, plus 2 tablespoons pickling liquid from the jar
2 tablespoons unsalted butter

For the Fish

4 (6-ounce) skin-on arctic char fillets
1 tablespoon extra-virgin olive oil
½ teaspoon kosher salt

1 MAKE THE BROWN BUTTER TOMATOES: In a high-powered blender, combine the cherry tomatoes, banana peppers, and their pickling liquid. Blend on low speed for about 30 seconds, or until the mixture is mostly liquefied but still with some pieces of tomato.

2 In a medium pan, melt the butter over high heat. When the butter begins to froth and sputter, reduce the heat to medium-low and cook, stirring, until it begins to brown, 2 to 3 minutes. Remove from the heat and let the butter cool slightly.

3 Add a spoonful of the tomato mixture to the browned butter: If the spattering is too aggressive, let the butter cool for another minute. Add the remaining tomato mixture and stir to combine. Return the pan to low heat and cover until the fish is done.

4 MAKE THE FISH: Line a large skillet with a piece of parchment paper. Covering the entire bottom of the pan.

5 Pat the skin side of the fillets dry, then drizzle over the olive oil and rub it into the skin. Season evenly with ¼ teaspoon of the salt. Place the fillets skin-side down into the pan on top of the parchment, ensuring all the skin touches the bottom of the pan. Season the flesh sides of the fish with the remaining ¼ teaspoon salt.

6 Place the pan over medium-high heat and cook until you begin to hear a sizzle, about 3 minutes, then reduce the heat to low, cover, and cook until the fish is opaque and an instant-read thermometer inserted into the thickest part of the fish reads 120°F for medium-rare, about 8 minutes, or longer if you prefer your fish cooked through.

7 Spoon the brown butter tomatoes into shallow bowls and top with the fish fillets, skin-side up. Serve.

Fish Tacos

Makes 8 tacos

For a quick dinner, few fish preparations are easier than these baked fish tacos. And when they're served family-style, everyone can pick the elements that they want. Because cod is so delicate, I went to town with the seasonings, but if you're like me and have a hot sauce collection, you can take it even further and line those bottles up! The mild fish also begs for texture to be added, and not doing so is a missed opportunity. The cabbage slaw here does fine work in checking that box, and any leftover cabbage can be used in the ruffage and bean recipe on page 102.

For the Fish Tacos

1 tablespoon extra-virgin olive oil
1½ teaspoons chopped garlic
¼ teaspoon dried oregano
½ teaspoon sweet paprika
¼ teaspoon kosher salt
⅛ teaspoon freshly ground black pepper
1 pound cod, cut into 2-inch pieces
¼ cup Pan-Fried Breadcrumbs (page 231) or store-bought seasoned breadcrumbs
8 (6-inch) flour tortillas

For the Cabbage Slaw

½ cup full-fat sour cream
¼ cup firmly packed fresh parsley
2 tablespoons fresh lime juice
¼ teaspoon honey
2 cups thinly sliced purple cabbage

For Serving

Hot sauce or Sweet & Zingy Fresno Chilies (page 230; optional)
2 limes, quartered

1 MAKE THE TACOS: Preheat the oven to 375°F. Line a baking sheet with parchment paper.

2 In a medium bowl, stir together the olive oil, garlic, oregano, paprika, salt, and pepper. Add the fish and toss, then add the breadcrumbs and toss until the fish is well coated. Arrange the fish in an even layer on the prepared baking sheet. Bake for 10 to 13 minutes, until the fish flakes apart with a fork.

3 MEANWHILE, MAKE THE SLAW: In a high-powered blender or food processor, combine the sour cream, parsley, lime juice, and honey. Blend on medium speed until smooth and light green, about 30 seconds. Transfer to a medium bowl. Add the cabbage and toss to coat well.

4 Working with one at a time, use tongs to hold the tortillas directly over a stovetop burner set to high. Cook until slightly charred and smoke just starts to wisp, 25 to 45 seconds per side. (Alternatively, you can do this in a cast-iron skillet over medium-high heat.)

5 To serve, place 1 or 2 pieces of the cod inside each tortilla. Top with the cabbage slaw and your favorite hot sauce or Fresno peppers, if desired, and serve with the lime quarters alongside.

Blackened Flounder

WITH TARRAGON ALMONDS

Serves 4

One of my favorite techniques in Cajun cuisine is blackening. Meat or fish is rubbed with a spice blend, then seared in a hot pan with butter until the spices blacken. They aren't burnt—just shy of that—and some say a lot of the color comes from the browning of the milk solids in the butter. Either way, when spices are cooked this way, they take on a commanding presence that I absolutely love. This flounder is spiced in that style and topped with butter-cooked almonds. The result is nutty, spicy, well seasoned, and easy!

- 3 tablespoons neutral oil
- 1 tablespoon fresh lemon juice
- 1 teaspoon Dijon mustard
- 1 tablespoon chopped fresh tarragon leaves
- 3 tablespoons unsalted butter
- ½ cup sliced almonds
- 1¼ teaspoons kosher salt
- 2 teaspoons hot paprika
- 2 teaspoons granulated garlic
- 1 teaspoon onion powder
- ½ teaspoon cayenne pepper
- ½ teaspoon freshly ground black pepper, plus more as needed
- 4 (6-ounce) skinless flounder fillets
- Flaky salt
- Red Pepper Olive Oil (page 226) or Calabrian chili oil

1 Position an oven rack 4 inches from the broiler heat source and preheat the broiler. Line a baking sheet with aluminum foil and drizzle the foil with 1½ tablespoons of the neutral oil.

2 In a small bowl, stir together the lemon juice, Dijon, and tarragon.

3 In a small skillet, melt the butter over medium heat. Add the almonds and ¼ teaspoon of the salt. Cook, stirring frequently, until the almonds are lightly golden brown, 3 to 5 minutes. Immediately transfer the almonds to the bowl with the lemon-mustard mixture and toss to coat.

4 In a separate small bowl, combine the hot paprika, granulated garlic, onion powder, cayenne, black pepper, and remaining 1 teaspoon salt. Stir well.

5 Place the flounder on the prepared baking sheet, then top the fish with the remaining 1½ tablespoons neutral oil. Using your hands, spread the oil evenly over the surface of the fish, then flip the fish over. Sprinkle the spice mix all over the fillets, dividing evenly.

6 Broil for 8 to 10 minutes, until the spices have darkened in some spots and the thickest part of the fish is firm to the touch. Remove from the oven and carefully transfer each fillet to a plate.

7 Scatter the almond mixture over the fish, sprinkle with flaky salt and more black pepper, and drizzle with red pepper olive oil, then serve immediately.

Roasted Flounder & Potatoes

Serves 4

Roasted potatoes and roasted fish are a wonderful pairing of simplicity and satisfaction. I'll never forget the whole branzino and potatoes I had in Venice—*indimenticabile*! Echoes of those moments came back when chef Michael Mina showed me his red snapper preparation with what he described as Egyptian mirepoix on top. What if thinly sliced potatoes and fish were roasted with a briny olive pâté topping? This is that, and it makes for an easy, complete fish dinner.

- 3 yellow potatoes (about 2 pounds), thinly sliced
- 4 tablespoons plus 1 teaspoon extra-virgin olive oil
- 1½ teaspoons kosher salt
- 1 small red onion, chopped
- ¼ cup pitted Kalamata olives
- ¼ cup sun-dried tomatoes
- 2 tablespoons tomato paste
- 1 teaspoon sweet paprika
- 4 (6-ounce) flounder fillets
- Chopped fresh parsley, for serving
- Lemon wedges, for serving

1 Position a rack in the center of the oven and preheat to 400°F. Line a baking sheet with parchment paper.

2 In a medium bowl, combine the potatoes, 3 tablespoons of the olive oil, and 1 teaspoon of the salt, toss to coat. Arrange the potatoes in a single layer on the prepared baking sheet, trying not to overlap. Pour any remaining oil from the bowl over the top.

3 Roast the potatoes for about 25 minutes, until they are cooked through, golden, and just beginning to brown in spots. Remove the potatoes, but keep the oven on.

4 In a food processor, combine the onion, olives, sun-dried tomatoes, tomato paste, 1 tablespoon of the olive oil, and paprika and process until smooth, about 45 seconds.

5 Arrange the flounder on top of the roasted potatoes. Drizzle with the remaining 1 teaspoon olive oil and season with the remaining ½ teaspoon salt, dividing it evenly. Spoon the olive-tomato mixture all over each fillet, spreading it into an even layer across the fish's surface.

6 Return the baking sheet to the oven and roast for about 10 minutes, or until the fish flakes easily with a fork or an instant-read thermometer inserted into the thickest part of the fish reaches 150°F.

7 Divide the potatoes and flounder among plates. Garnish with the parsley and serve with lemon wedges alongside for squeezing.

DRINKS

Nonno's Martini

Makes 2 drinks

My nonno Frank, for whom I was named, had a serious passion for cooking. Many of my first experiences with multicourse fine dining happened at my grandparents' house. When I was still the only grandchild, the meals would end with espresso spiked with a small amount of sambuca, a licorice-flavored liqueur. I'd sit on his lap and ask, "Nonno, can I have the coffee with the 'stuff' in it?" and he'd let me sip a teaspoon. This is my first-ever food memory, and any time I have a *caffe coretto*, as the Italians call it, I'm transported. Nonno passed away before I could truly enjoy his adult beverages, but my other grandfather, Pappa Nick, used to make me Nonno Frank's martini. The secret is a capful of Scotch. It is gloriously smooth, and I hope you enjoy it as much as I do. If you're thinking about swapping the gin for vodka, you can, but first I want you to know that gin *is* vodka. That's right: Gin is vodka infused with juniper berries, so I encourage you to try it, or try it again if it's been a while.

3 ounces dry gin
¾ ounce dry vermouth
¾ ounce olive brine
½ ounce Scotch
6 pitted martini olives

1 In a cocktail shaker or mason jar with a lid, combine the gin, vermouth, olive brine, Scotch, and a few ice cubes. Shake vigorously for 30 seconds.

2 Strain into two martini glasses, dividing the drink evenly. Garnish each cocktail with 3 martini olives.

Blueberry Thyme Shrub

Serves 8 to 10

This is another drink that I learned while filming *Struggle Meals*, and frankly too late in life. A shrub is a sort of vinegar-soda syrup slightly reminiscent of kombucha. It takes a week to make, but it's a perfect way to use up blueberries if you have too many. Straining the thyme out of the shrub after the fermentation period will make this last for a month or more. Add it to seltzer, beer, or sparkling white wine, or, if you're feeling brave, drink it straight with ice—that's how I like it!

1 pound fresh blueberries
1½ cups sugar
½ cup packed fresh thyme leaves (from 1 bunch), plus thyme sprigs for garnish (if desired)
½ cup apple cider vinegar
½ cup sherry vinegar
Club soda or seltzer, for serving

1 In a large airtight container, use a muddler or a potato masher to combine the blueberries and sugar, crushing the fruit and sugar together but leaving the mixture a little bit chunky. Cover and refrigerate overnight.

2 The next day, remove the mixture from the fridge and stir in the thyme and vinegars. Cover again and refrigerate for 7 to 10 days to infuse, stirring it once a day. The mixture will smell bright and vinegary and should be free of any scum or white discoloration.

3 Set a fine-mesh sieve over a large bowl and strain the mixture through it, discarding any solids. Transfer the liquid to a clean airtight container and store in the refrigerator for up to 1 month.

4 To enjoy, add 2 ounces to an ice-filled glass, top with club soda, and garnish with thyme sprigs, if desired.

Beermosa

Makes 4 drinks

Sparkling white wine with orange juice is the perfect example of a drink that can be so great or so horrible, depending on the quality of the ingredients. Mimosas are, however, forever banished in my mind, because I worked the brunch shift and I saw the rowdy monsters the "bottomless" offering created in the dining room! So here's a beermosa, which, funny enough, I like to make with nonalcoholic beers, a category that has exploded with fantastic options in the 2020s. With alcohol or without, it's bubbly, festive, and, when combined with truly freshly squeezed orange juice, perfect. Let's raise a glass to being mellow this brunch.

4 (12-ounce) bottles light beer, such as Corona, or nonalcoholic beer, such as Peroni 0.0
16 ounces fresh orange juice

1 Pour a bottle of beer into each of four glasses.

2 Top each with 4 ounces of the orange juice.

Sour Tequila

Makes 2 drinks

This drink is all my wife Heather's creation; she's a master of embracing both sweet and sour in drinks, dressings, and life. Her inspiration was something between a margarita and a whiskey sour, and the result is smooth, clean, and perfectly balanced. When friends come over for brick chicken (see page 138), we start with this cocktail, and it's always delicious.

- 1 tablespoon Tajín, for rimming the glasses
- 1 teaspoon sugar, for rimming the glasses
- 1 lime wedge, for rimming the glasses
- 3 ounces blanco tequila
- ¾ ounce Cointreau
- ¾ ounce fresh lime juice
- ½ ounce pure maple syrup
- ½ ounce Amarena syrup
- 2 Amarena cherries

1 On a shallow plate, stir together the Tajín and sugar. Run a lime wedge around the rim of a coupe, then dip the rim into the Tajín mixture to coat. Repeat with a second coupe glass.

2 In a cocktail shaker or mason jar with a lid, combine the tequila, Cointreau, lime juice, maple syrup, Amarena syrup, and a few ice cubes. Shake vigorously for 30 seconds. Strain into the prepared glasses, dividing the drink evenly. Garnish each cocktail with a cherry and enjoy immediately.

Mountain Toddy

Makes 4 drinks

On a cold winter day, or when I'm under the weather, a hot toddy is my go-to. There are many variations, but a toddy can be as simple as boiling water with lemon, cloves, and bourbon. This recipe takes it a little further, steeping a maple and sage "tea" to extract the flavors of what tastes to me like a mossy mountain's base. So whether you're well but chilly, or unwell and need to warm up, the mountain toddy will heal your ills.

3 ounces pure maple syrup
15 to 20 fresh sage leaves
1 (3-inch) strip of lemon peel
1 (6-inch) strip of orange peel
6 ounces bourbon
Orange slices, for garnish

1 In a small saucepan, combine 3 cups water, the maple syrup, sage, and lemon and orange peels. Bring to a gentle boil over medium heat, then reduce the heat to low, cover, and simmer for about 20 minutes, until the flavors have melded and the liquid turns a pale yellow color. Place a fine-mesh sieve over a spouted measuring cup and strain the infused liquid. Discard the solids.

2 Pour 1½ ounces of the bourbon into each of four mugs, then add the infused liquid, dividing it evenly. Stir to combine, garnish with orange slices, and serve immediately.

Bloody Beer

Makes 4 drinks

The umami-filled Bloody Mary is unique, and I thought it stood alone in the savory and filling drink category. But I was wrong. When I started dating my wife, she made me aware of two relatives of the Bloody Mary: the Bull Shot (vodka and beef bouillon) and the Bloody Bull, a beef bouillon–laden Bloody Mary. These days, vodka is just too strong for me, and by combining the best elements of a Bloody Bull with beer (or nonalcoholic beer), I was able to make a classic that won't knock you out. Batch it for a crowd or make them individually.

¼ cup Old Bay seasoning, for rimming the glasses
2 lemon wedges, for rimming the glasses
2 (12-ounce) bottles lager or pilsner (or nonalcoholic beer, such as Peroni 0.0)
3 (5.5-ounce) cans tomato juice, such as V8
3 tablespoons fresh lemon juice
4 ounces beef consommé, such as Campbell's
1 teaspoon freshly ground black pepper

For Serving

12 ice cubes
4 celery stalks
4 blue cheese–stuffed olives
4 Peppadew peppers
4 pimento-stuffed olives
Hot sauce

1 Spread the Old Bay over a shallow plate. Rub a lemon wedge around the rim of a pint glass, then dip the rim in the Old Bay to coat. Repeat with three more pint glasses.

2 In a pitcher or other large container, combine the beer, tomato juice, lemon juice, consommé, and black pepper. Stir to combine.

3 Place 3 ice cubes in each prepared glass, then fill them with the bloody beer. Garnish each glass with a celery rib and a toothpick skewered with a blue cheese olive, a Peppadew pepper, and a pimento-stuffed olive. Finish with hot sauce to taste.

Two-for-One Sangria

Makes 6 drinks

I wanted to make a slushy drink, which proved harder than I thought it would be. But at every pass, the sangria from the blender was fantastic, so I ended up with a two-for-one. The sangria can be served immediately, or it can be popped into the freezer and served as a slushy cocktail later. Although the alcohol prevents it from freezing into a solid block of ice, it's a good idea to run a fork through the sangria every few hours to prevent any large ice clumps from forming.

½ cup sugar
1 (750ml) bottle fruity Spanish red wine, such as tempranillo or garnacha
¼ cup brandy
3 cups frozen mixed berries
2 cups ice cubes, plus more as needed

1 In a small saucepan, combine ½ cup water and the sugar. Bring to a boil over medium heat, stirring occasionally. When the sugar has melted, transfer the mixture to a small heatproof bowl and place in the freezer to cool completely, about 20 minutes.

2 Transfer the cooled syrup to a high-powered blender and add the wine, brandy, berries, and ice. Blend on high speed until the fruit has completely broken down, about 1 minute.

3 If serving immediately, pour the sangria into glasses with ice, if desired (see Note), and enjoy.

4 To make slushy sangria, pour the sangria into quart containers, cover, and freeze for at least 5 hours. Divide the slushy sangria among glasses and serve immediately.

NOTE: If you're serving the sangria immediately, you can add more ice to reduce the perceived sweetness. If freezing overnight, the perceived sweetness will naturally mellow out, so adding more ice before serving isn't recommended.

Moka Martini

Makes 4 drinks

The espresso martini is a high-octane beverage, and I've always felt that its purpose of delivering maximum caffeine and alcohol took precedence over tasting good. Enter the Moka Martini, which has nothing to do with chocolate and everything to do with tasting better. Let's break it down: A moka pot is the affordable stovetop coffee maker that every household in Italy uses. They're widely available, dead simple to use, and make great, strong coffee. It's the perfect brew for a moka martini, in which the vodka has been pared back and the coffee liqueur increased—all in the name of flavor!

1 cup hot coffee (preferably brewed in a moka pot)
1 tablespoon sugar
3 ounces vodka
1½ ounces coffee liqueur, such as Kahlúa
6 ice cubes

1 In a cocktail shaker, combine the hot coffee and sugar and stir vigorously until the sugar has dissolved, about 20 seconds. Add the vodka, coffee liqueur, and ice cubes. Shake vigorously until the shaker is ice cold to the touch, about 1 minute.

2 Strain into four martini glasses, dividing the drink evenly, and serve.

La Bicicletta

Serves 8 to 10

This is my all-time favorite summer drink. At first glance, it may come across as just another Campari spritz, but it's so much more than that. As a teen, I competed in road and track cycling at the national level—and I'm still in love with the sport to this day. To then have a drink named "The Bicycle" is just the best. In all sports, athletes search for an advantage; in cycling, that edge has taken on a lot of different forms. For example, early photos of the Tour de France depict cyclists climbing the Alps while smoking cigarettes, which they thought made them faster. But the legend of the Bici (the nickname of La Bicicletta) is that Gino Bartali, one of Italy's most accomplished cyclists, used to ride with this drink in his bike's bottle cage. It's not just a spritz—there's sparking water in the drink as well, so it's hydrating and buzz-creating at the same time. It's a refreshing large-batch cocktail that's perfect for climbing the Dolomites. Or for maintaining a fantastic time in the sun, all day long.

1 (750ml) bottle Prosecco
3 cups sparkling water, such as San Pellegrino, plus more if needed
2 cups Campari, plus more if needed
2 limes, halved
2 lemons, halved

1 In a large pitcher or other vessel, combine the Prosecco, sparkling water, and Campari. Squeeze in the juice of the limes and lemons, then drop in the spent rinds. Add plenty of ice and give everything a gentle stir so as to not disturb the bubbles too much.

2 Fill large tumblers with ice and ladle in the bici. Add more Campari to make it stronger or more sparkling water to make it more hydrating.

The Necromancer

Makes 4 drinks

There's just something so refreshing yet unexpected about this cocktail. If you haven't yet purchased a bottle of Lillet Blanc and/or St-Germain, I highly recommend doing so, even if just for this recipe. (You're going to want to make it all the time, I promise.) Each brings a fresh and floral sweetness, and both drink well on their own with just an ice cube. This recipe is best served shaken until "frothy," with the vodka poured straight from the freezer and the Lillet and St-Germain prechilled, which is made easy by storing them in the fridge.

4 ounces Lillet Blanc
4 ounces vodka
1 ounce St-Germain elderflower liqueur
1 ounce fresh lemon juice
8 ice cubes
4 lemon twists, for garnish

1 In a cocktail shaker, combine the Lillet Blanc, vodka, St-Germain, lemon juice, and ice cubes. Shake vigorously until the shaker is ice cold to the touch, about 1 minute.

2 Strain into four cocktail glasses, dividing the drink evenly, and garnish with a lemon twist before serving.

SWEETS

Chocolate Cherry Brownies

Makes 12 brownies

Brownies are a great place to start if you're new to baking. You have to follow directions, but nothing is difficult. There's hand-mixing, which is great to get kids involved, and as the brownies bake, everyone knows what's coming: a delicious treat! These brownies are made unique with dark cherries, which cut through some of the chocolaty richness while bringing unexpected—but welcome—fresh, deep, dark fruitiness.

Nonstick cooking spray
½ cup (1 stick/120g) unsalted butter
8 ounces dark chocolate (at least 70% cacao), coarsely chopped
¾ cup (135g) packed light brown sugar
½ cup (100g) granulated sugar
1 large egg yolk
3 large eggs
1 teaspoon almond extract
½ teaspoon pure vanilla extract
¾ cup (90g) all-purpose flour
½ teaspoon kosher salt
20 dark cherries, such as Bing, pitted and halved
¼ cup semisweet chocolate chips

1 Preheat the oven to 350°F. Coat an 8-inch square baking pan with cooking spray and line with parchment paper.

2 In a medium heatproof bowl, combine the butter and chocolate. Microwave in 30-second increments, stirring after each, until completely melted. Let cool slightly.

3 Add the brown sugar and granulated sugar to the butter-chocolate mixture and whisk vigorously until the sugar is mostly dissolved, about 2 minutes. Whisk in the egg yolk, followed by the eggs, one at a time, being sure each addition is fully incorporated before adding the next. Whisk in the almond extract and vanilla. Add the flour and salt and gently fold to combine. (Take care not to overmix—a few dry streaks are okay.) Fold in the cherries.

4 Transfer the brownie batter to the prepared pan. Sprinkle the chocolate chips over the top. Bake for 35 minutes, or until the surface of the brownies is crackly and shiny, with no jiggle to the center of the brownies. Transfer to a wire rack and let cool for 1 hour, then transfer to the refrigerator to cool completely, 1 hour more.

5 Slice the brownies into 12 squares and serve. Store in an airtight container at room temperature for up to 5 days.

Miso Snickerdoodle Ice Cream Sandwiches

Makes 18 individual cookies or 9 ice cream sandwiches

These cookies are wonderful on their own. The miso gives a subtly salty umami that also adds to the chew in mysterious ways. But when you sandwich vanilla ice cream between two cookies, the miso pops even more—and their texture is perfect even after days in the freezer. Making the sandwiches all in one batch can be challenging, just because ice cream melts—and you certainly don't have to turn all the cookies into sandwiches. So mix, match, and enjoy these delights however you like!

- 1½ cups plus 3 tablespoons (300g) sugar
- ½ cup (1 stick/115g) unsalted butter, at room temperature
- ½ cup (95g) vegetable shortening
- ¼ cup (7g) white miso paste
- 2 large eggs, at room temperature
- 2 teaspoons pure vanilla extract
- 3 cups (390g) all-purpose flour
- 2 teaspoons cream of tartar
- 1 teaspoon baking soda
- ½ teaspoon kosher salt
- 1 tablespoon ground cinnamon

- 1 pint vanilla ice cream

1 In the bowl of a stand mixer fitted with the paddle attachment, combine 1½ cups of the sugar, the butter, shortening, and miso. Mix on medium speed to incorporate, about 1 minute, then mix on medium-high until pale yellow and fluffy, 5 to 8 minutes. Add the eggs and vanilla and mix on medium to incorporate, 1 minute more.

2 In a medium bowl, whisk together the flour, cream of tartar, baking soda, and salt. Add the dry ingredients to the wet and mix on low until just barely combined, about 20 seconds.

3 Line two baking sheets with parchment paper. Roll the cookie dough into 18 equal balls, slightly larger than a golf ball, and place on the prepared baking sheets. Refrigerate, uncovered, for at least 1 hour, or tightly wrapped in plastic for up to 24 hours.

4 Preheat the oven to 375°F. Line another baking sheet with parchment.

5 In a small bowl, stir together the remaining 3 tablespoons sugar and the cinnamon. Roll each dough ball in the mixture. Place the cookies on the baking sheet you just prepared, spacing them about 4 inches apart. (Refrigerate the remaining dough balls until ready to bake.)

6 Bake for 8 to 12 minutes, until the edges are barely golden brown and the cookies are puffy and cracks appear down the middle. Let cool on the baking sheet for 5 minutes, then transfer to a wire rack to cool completely. (The cooled cookies can be stored in an airtight container at room temperature for up to 5 days.)

7 To make ice cream sandwiches, scoop about 2 tablespoons of vanilla ice cream onto the flat side of 9 cookies. Top with the remaining cookies, flat-side down, then freeze on a clean baking sheet for a least 1 hour to firm up before serving. Individually wrap the ice cream sandwiches in foil and place in a resealable bag. Store in the freezer for up to 1 month.

Spiced Sweet Potato Cake

WITH NUTMEG MASCARPONE FROSTING

Serves 6 to 10

I don't know how to tell you this, but this cake was inspired by a sweet potato dessert I was served on a long-haul flight. Plane food can be gross—this was anything but. Sweet potato pairs incredibly well with warming spices like nutmeg, allspice, and cinnamon. It's like a carrot cake, but lighter, and I like to use mascarpone instead of the traditional cream cheese to keep the theme of "lighter" going.

For the Spiced Sweet Potato Cake

- 2 to 3 large sweet potatoes
- Nonstick cooking spray
- 1 cup (200g) granulated sugar
- ½ cup (90g) packed dark brown sugar
- 5 large eggs, at room temperature
- 1 cup vegetable oil
- 2 teaspoons pure vanilla extract
- 3 cups (360g) all-purpose flour
- 2 teaspoons baking powder
- 2 teaspoons ground cinnamon
- 1 teaspoon kosher salt
- ¼ teaspoon ground ginger
- ¼ teaspoon ground cloves
- ¼ teaspoon ground allspice

For the Nutmeg Mascarpone Frosting

- 8 ounces mascarpone, at room temperature
- 1 (8-ounce) block full-fat cream cheese, at room temperature
- 1 teaspoon freshly grated nutmeg, plus more for garnish
- ½ teaspoon pure vanilla extract
- ½ teaspoon ground cinnamon
- ¼ cup plus 2 tablespoons confectioners' sugar

1 **MAKE THE CAKE:** Bring a medium pot of water to a boil over high heat. Add the potatoes and cook until fork-tender, 30 to 45 minutes. Drain and let cool, then peel the potatoes and place the flesh in a medium bowl. Use a potato masher or fork to mash; measure out 3 cups.

2 Preheat the oven to 350°F. Coat two 9-inch round cake pans with nonstick spray, then line the bottoms with parchment paper cut to fit and spray the parchment as well.

3 In the bowl of a stand mixer fitted with the paddle attachment, beat both sugars with the eggs on medium-high speed, scraping down the sides as necessary, until pale in color and fluffy, about 5 minutes. Add the oil and beat on medium to combine, about 2 minutes. Add the mashed sweet potatoes and vanilla and beat on low, scraping down the sides as needed, until combined, 1 to 2 minutes.

4 In a medium bowl, whisk together the flour, baking powder, cinnamon, salt, ginger, cloves, and allspice. Add the dry ingredients to the wet and beat on low until just barely combined, about 2 minutes.

5 Divide the batter evenly between the prepared pans. Bake for about 30 minutes, until a toothpick inserted into the center of the cakes comes out with moist crumbs attached. Let cool in the pans for 10 minutes, then remove from the pans and transfer to a wire rack to cool completely.

6 **MEANWHILE, MAKE THE FROSTING:** In the bowl of a stand mixer fitted with the paddle attachment, combine the mascarpone, cream cheese, nutmeg, vanilla, cinnamon, and confectioners' sugar. Mix on low speed until combined, about 3 minutes.

7 Place one cake layer on a serving platter. Use a long serrated knife to level the top horizontally. Spread half the frosting evenly over the top, stopping at the edges. Add the second cake layer and top with the remaining frosting. Garnish with a bit of nutmeg, slice, and serve. Store, covered, at room temperature for up to 2 days or in the refrigerator for up to 5 days.

Chocolate Peanut Butter Rice Cereal Treats

Makes 12 treats

I love a Rice Krispies Treat; sometimes I'll take them with me as an energy bar on longer bike rides. Here I topped them with the classic combination of peanut butter and chocolate and finished them with some chopped sweet dates and flaky salt for an "all ages welcome" dessert.

- Nonstick cooking spray
- 1 (10-ounce) bag mini marshmallows
- ½ cup creamy peanut butter
- 4 tablespoons (½ stick) unsalted butter
- ½ teaspoon kosher salt
- 5 cups puffed rice cereal
- 1½ cups semisweet or dark chocolate chips
- 6 small dates, pitted and chopped
- Flaky salt

1 Coat a 9-inch square baking pan with nonstick spray.

2 In a large saucepan, combine the marshmallows, peanut butter, butter, and salt over medium-low heat. Let the butter melt slowly, then gently fold everything together and cook, stirring, until the ingredients have all melted and are well combined, about 2 minutes. Remove the pan from the heat, add the rice cereal, and mix well. Transfer to the prepared pan and gently press into the edges.

3 In a medium microwave-safe bowl, heat the chocolate chips in the microwave in 30-second increments, stirring between each. Pour the melted chocolate over the cereal treats and smooth out the top. Sprinkle the chocolate with dates and flaky salt. Refrigerate until the chocolate has completely hardened, about 1 hour.

4 To serve, coat a knife with nonstick spray and cut into 12 squares. Store leftover treats in an airtight container in the refrigerator for up to 5 days.

Ricotta Maple Cheesecake

Serves 12

This cheesecake was inspired by the Blue Dolphin Diner in Katonah, New York, a wonderful Italian restaurant run by a couple from the island of Capri since the 1980s. A meal there is always a great idea. Desserts are displayed in a glass refrigerator next to the bar, an old-school move that I wish more restaurants still did. Alfredo's cheesecake is light and made with ricotta, which got me thinking: Could I lighten up the Spanish Basque cheesecake by taking some cues from the Blue Dolphin? Yes, and it works!

- Nonstick cooking spray
- 2 pounds (905g) whole-milk ricotta cheese
- 2 (8-ounce/225g) blocks full-fat cream cheese, at room temperature
- ½ cup (100g) sugar
- ½ cup (160g) pure maple syrup
- 1½ teaspoons pure vanilla extract
- 1 teaspoon kosher salt
- 7 large eggs

1 Preheat the oven to 425°F. Coat a 9-inch springform pan with nonstick spray, then line the pan with parchment paper. (No need to be fussy: Two 15-inch-long pieces of parchment placed in an X pattern should cover the bottom and sides of the pan well. The folds that form in the corners of the parchment are fine and yield a rustic edge to the cake that I like.)

2 In the bowl of a stand mixer fitted with the whisk attachment, combine the ricotta and cream cheese. Mix on low speed until evenly combined, about 1 minute. Scrape down the sides of the bowl, then add the sugar, maple syrup, vanilla, and salt. Mix on low speed until incorporated, 1 to 2 minutes. Scrape down the sides of the bowl again, add the eggs all at once, and mix on low speed until the batter is well combined, 2 to 3 minutes more.

3 Pour the batter into the prepared pan. Tap the bottom of the pan against the counter to release any bubbles.

4 Bake for 30 to 40 minutes, or until the edges of the cheesecake begin to set and gently brown. Reduce the heat to 375°F and bake for 40 to 50 minutes more, or until the cheesecake turns amber brown on the surface and the middle jiggles but is no longer liquid.

5 Transfer the cheesecake to a wire rack and let cool in the pan to room temperature, 1 to 2 hours. Set the cheesecake (still in the pan!) on a plate and refrigerate, uncovered, for at least 4 hours, or until the cheesecake has fully set. (Once set, the cheesecake can be covered and stored in the fridge for up to 4 days.)

6 Remove the ring from the springform pan, slice the cheesecake, and serve.

Coconut Poke Cake

Serves 12

I love coconut everything, but didn't know I needed coconut cake in my life—that is, until I tried the perfection that the pastry team at Stissing House in Pine Plains, New York, has achieved. Since that first bite, I've been on a quest to eat all the coconut cake possible and in the process realized that it is the perfect "plain" cake. In my recipe, a moist plain cake is poked with holes which allows all the liquid coconut to soak inside. It's light, rich, clean and spiced all at the same time. Serve it alone or with vanilla ice cream. Delicacy!

- Nonstick cooking spray
- ¾ cup (1½ sticks) unsalted butter, at room temperature
- 1 cup (200g) granulated sugar
- 3 large eggs, at room temperature
- 1 teaspoon vanilla extract
- 2 cups (255g) cake flour
- ¼ teaspoon kosher salt
- 1 tablespoon baking powder
- ⅔ cup whole milk, at room temperature
- ⅔ cup coconut milk
- ¼ cup sweetened condensed milk
- 1 cup cold heavy cream
- 1 teaspoon powdered sugar
- ½ teaspoon ground cinnamon
- ¼ cup coconut flakes, toasted

1 Preheat the oven to 350°F. Coat a 9 × 13-inch baking dish with nonstick spray. Line the bottom with parchment paper cut to fit, then spray the parchment as well.

2 In the bowl of a stand mixer fitted with the paddle attachment, cream the butter and granulated sugar on medium-high speed until pale, about 3 minutes. Add the eggs one at a time, beating until each is completely incorporated before adding the next, then beat in the vanilla. Turn off the mixer.

3 In a medium bowl, whisk together the cake flour, salt, and baking powder to combine. Add half the flour mixture to the mixer bowl and mix on low to combine. Add the whole milk and mix until combined. Add the remaining flour mixture and mix until combined.

4 Scrape the batter into the prepared baking dish and spread it evenly. Bake for 25 to 30 minutes, until the top of the cake is golden all over. Remove from the oven and transfer to a wire rack to cool slightly.

5 Meanwhile, in a spouted measuring cup, stir together the coconut milk and condensed milk.

6 Use a skewer to poke holes over the entire surface of the warm cake, spacing them about ¼ inch apart. Slowly pour the coconut milk mixture over the cake, stopping periodically to let the cake absorb the liquid. Let the cake cool to room temperature, about 45 minutes.

7 In the bowl of a stand mixer fitted with the whisk attachment, whip the heavy cream on medium-high speed until it just starts to aerate, about 1 minute, then add the powdered sugar and whip until soft peaks form, 1 to 2 minutes more.

8 Dollop the whipped cream over the top of the cake and gently spread it to the edges. Dust with the cinnamon, then finish with the toasted coconut. Cut into 12 squares and serve immediately. Store leftovers, covered, at room temperature for up to 1 day or in the refrigerator for up to 5 days.

Banana Pull-Apart Bread

Serves 6 to 8

The first thing I ever cooked with my mom was banana bread; I'd lick the battered whisks, as one does, and stare through the oven window in amazement as the thick liquid turned into something that a knife could cut. Bananas are here for my, and hopefully your, nostalgia, but everything else about this dessert is new age. It's an upside-down cake (okay, maybe that's vintage), it uses biscuit dough (makes life easier), and the whole thing is held together with molten banana syrup. You can have a portion as small as a doughnut hole or a cluster of several. I haven't used the word "addictive" yet, but I will now, because that's what this is.

- Nonstick cooking spray
- ¼ cup sugar
- 1 tablespoon ground cinnamon
- 2 (16-ounce) cans refrigerated biscuits
- 1 cup packed dark brown sugar
- ½ cup (1 stick) butter, melted
- 3 very ripe bananas, cut into 2-inch pieces
- 1 teaspoon pure vanilla extract
- 1 teaspoon kosher salt
- ½ cup chopped walnuts

1 Preheat the oven to 350°F. Coat a 9-inch round cake pan with nonstick spray. Line the bottom with parchment paper cut to fit and spray the parchment as well.

2 In a large bowl, whisk together sugar and cinnamon. Separate the biscuits and cut each into 4 pieces. Add the pieces to the bowl and gently toss to coat well.

3 In a medium bowl, combine the brown sugar, melted butter, bananas, vanilla, and salt. Use a potato masher or whisk to mash the bananas into small pieces and incorporate them.

4 Add half of the biscuit pieces to the bottom of the prepared pan. Sprinkle half of the walnuts over the top, followed by half of the banana mixture. Add the remaining biscuits, followed by more walnuts, and the rest of the banana mixture.

5 Place the pan on a baking sheet. Bake for 50 to 70 minutes, or until the biscuits are deeply golden brown and the middle is no longer liquidy but still jiggles slightly. Remove from the oven and let cool in the pan for 10 minutes.

6 Loosen the sides of the bread with an offset spatula or a knife. Invert the pan onto a large plate to release the bread. Serve immediately. Store covered at room temperature for up to 2 days or in the refrigerator for up to 5 days. Reheat in the microwave on 50% power in 2-minute increments until warmed through.

Anise Biscotti

Makes 8

When you think of biscotti, you might think of cute little buttery biscuits flavored with almonds. Or maybe you imagine a drier and less-sweet baked good, with an anise licorice flavor to them. The latter is the style of biscotti I grew up with, the kind Mom made special trips to buy, a style that's nearly extinct. Today's biscotti overwhelmingly have a lot of butter and sugar, which is fine, until you dip one into coffee or tea and it disintegrates. But these anise biscotti hold up, and they make a lovely breakfast or post-dinner treat.

- 2 tablespoons unsalted butter, at room temperature
- ½ cup plus 2 tablespoons (150g) sugar
- 2 large eggs
- 1 teaspoon pure vanilla extract
- 2 cups plus 3 tablespoons (280g) all-purpose flour, plus more if needed
- ½ teaspoon kosher salt
- ¼ teaspoon baking powder
- 2 teaspoons ground star anise (about 3 stars, pulverized in a high-powered blender)

1 Preheat the oven to 350°F. Line a baking sheet with parchment paper.

2 In the bowl of a stand mixer fitted with the paddle attachment, or in a medium bowl using a handheld mixer, beat the butter, sugar, eggs, and vanilla on high speed until pale yellow and smooth, about 4 minutes.

3 In a medium bowl, whisk together the flour, salt, baking powder, and star anise. Add the dry ingredients to the wet ingredients and mix on low speed until the ingredients just come together, about 1 minute. The dough should be pasty and a little bit sticky. If it's too sticky to handle, add more flour 1 teaspoon at a time.

4 Turn the dough out onto the prepared baking sheet. Use your hands to pat it down into a roughly 6-inch square, about 1 inch thick. Taper the top and bottom edges to create a loaflike shape. (It should look like classic biscotti from the side.)

5 Bake the loaf for 30 minutes until the top just begins to darken, then remove from the oven and let it rest for about 15 minutes, or until it's cool enough to handle. Keep the oven on.

6 Cut the loaf in half along the direction of the taper. Then cut 4 equal-size biscotti from each half, for a total of 8. Return the biscotti to the baking sheet, oriented as they were before being cut, but space them at least an inch apart. Return to the oven and bake for 20 minutes, or until the cut sides of the cookies are fully cooked.

7 Let the biscotti cool completely on the baking sheet. Store in an airtight container at room temperature for up to 1 week.

Key Lime Pretzel Icebox Pie

Serves 8

An icebox cake is a semi-homemade frozen treat that significantly lowers the bar to entry into the world of homemade desserts. This recipe sports a crust made of crushed mini pretzels (so tasty!), and the filling can be made with Persian limes or key limes. Expect an intriguingly bright and cool pie, with a welcome salty crunch to each bite.

For the Crust

3 cups mini pretzels
¼ cup sugar
½ cup (1 stick) unsalted butter, melted

For the Filling

1 (8-ounce) block full-fat cream cheese, at room temperature
1 (14-ounce) can sweetened condensed milk
¾ cup fresh key lime juice or lime juice (from about 15 key limes or 6 limes)
1 (8-ounce) container whipped topping
1 tablespoon key lime zest or lime zest

1 **MAKE THE CRUST:** In a food processor, combine the pretzels and sugar and process until the pretzels take on a texture similar to breadcrumbs, about 2 minutes. With the motor running, slowly stream in the melted butter and process until the mixture forms large clumps, about 1 minute more.

2 Transfer the mixture to a 9-inch pie pan. Using the heel of your palm or the bottom of a measuring cup, press the crust into the pie pan and up the sides, being sure to keep it flat and even.

3 **MAKE THE FILLING:** Wipe out the food processor bowl and add the cream cheese, sweetened condensed milk, and lime juice. Process until smooth and fully combined, about 1 minute. Transfer the mixture to a large bowl. Add the whipped topping and gently fold to combine.

4 Pour the filling into the crust, smoothing it out evenly. Sprinkle the zest over the top, then freeze overnight or until the filling has solidified. Remove from the freezer and slice and serve immediately.

Orange Curd & Pistachio Shortbread Bars

Serves 4 to 8

Citrus curd and shortbread are a match made in heaven. They're a wonderful example of how acidity can allow your taste buds to take even more sweetness, fat, and savoriness without being overwhelmed. In this recipe, the sweet acidity of orange curd is set atop pistachio shortbread. It's everything you imagine it will be, and a great dessert to make ahead when you're having company over.

Nonstick cooking spray

For the Pistachio Shortbread

⅓ cup (50g) shelled pistachios
1 cup (120g) all-purpose flour
¼ cup (65g) granulated sugar
½ cup (1 stick/120g) unsalted butter, melted

For the Orange Curd

1 cup (200g) granulated sugar
2 tablespoons orange zest
¼ cup (30g) all-purpose flour
¼ teaspoon kosher salt
3 large eggs
⅓ cup fresh orange juice
3 tablespoons fresh lemon juice

Confectioners' sugar, for dusting (optional)

1 Preheat the oven to 325°F. Grease an 8-inch square glass baking dish with cooking spray and line with overhanging parchment paper.

2 **MAKE THE SHORTBREAD:** Place the pistachios in a food processor and process until finely ground (a few larger pieces are okay), about 2 minutes. Add the flour and granulated sugar and pulse several times just to combine. Add the melted butter and pulse to achieve a crumbly, slightly wet dough.

3 Transfer the dough to the prepared baking dish and use the heel of your palm or the bottom of a measuring cup to press the crust evenly into the bottom of the pan. Place in the freezer for at least 15 minutes until the dough is firm, or up to 1 hour while you make the curd.

4 Bake the crust for about 25 minutes, until lightly golden brown around the edges. Remove from the oven.

5 **MEANWHILE, MAKE THE CURD:** In a medium bowl, combine the sugar and orange zest. Using your fingertips, rub the zest and granulated sugar together until fragrant. Add the flour and salt and whisk to incorporate. Whisk in the eggs, then the orange and lemon juices. Pour the mixture over the warm crust. Lightly tap the bottom of the baking dish against the counter to release any air bubbles.

6 Bake for about 35 minutes, or until mostly set but the center still jiggles slightly. Transfer to a wire rack to let cool to room temperature, about 1 hour, then cover and place in the refrigerator to cool completely, about 3 hours.

7 Once the bars have cooled completely, dust the top with confectioners' sugar, if you'd like. Using the overhanging parchment as handles, remove from the baking dish and cut into squares, rectangles, or wedges. Store in an airtight container in the refrigerator for up to 5 days.

Caramel Banana Tiracisu

Serves 12 to 15

The original tiramisu is an undisputed classic. Its name is actually two words jammed together: *tirami* and *su*, which translates to "pick me up." With espresso, sugar, chocolate, and fresh raw eggs, it does just that. For me, the dessert has always sounded a little lonely, which is why I made a sharable version that I'm calling *tiracisu*, or "pick *us* up." The coffee remains, and my love for bananas is projected into this large-format, no-raw-egg, caramel delight.

½ cup (1 stick) unsalted butter
1 cup sugar
2 cups cold heavy cream
½ teaspoon kosher salt
3 ripe bananas, thinly sliced
2 (3.4-ounce) boxes instant vanilla pudding
4 cups cold whole milk
1 teaspoon pure vanilla extract
2 cups coffee, at room temperature or colder
1 (14-ounce) package ladyfingers

1 In a 12-inch skillet, melt the butter over medium heat. Cook, swirling the pan occasionally, until browned, about 3 minutes. Add the sugar and swirl the pan again to combine. Cook, stirring occasionally, until the sugar darkens, 3 minutes more.

2 Reduce the heat to low, then carefully add 1 cup of the heavy cream and the salt; the mixture will sputter. Stir to combine, then add the bananas and stir until combined. Cook until the bananas have absorbed a bit of the caramel and are glossy, about 2 minutes. Remove from the heat.

3 Meanwhile, in the bowl of a stand mixer fitted with the whisk attachment, combine the pudding mix and milk. Whip on medium speed until well combined and thickened, about 2 minutes. Transfer the pudding to a medium bowl and set aside to thicken further, about 5 minutes.

4 Add the remaining 1 cup heavy cream and the vanilla to the stand mixer bowl (no need to wipe it out). Whip on medium-high speed until stiff peaks form, 4 to 6 minutes. Add the whipped cream to the pudding mixture and use a rubber spatula to fold gently.

5 Pour the chilled coffee into a shallow bowl. Add 1 ladyfinger at a time, soaking it for 1 second, then flipping it over and soaking it for another second. Transfer the ladyfingers to a 9 × 13-inch baking dish, repeating until the bottom of the pan is completely covered.

6 Add half of the vanilla cream to the baking dish and spread it evenly over the ladyfingers to the edges of the pan. Top with half of the banana caramel and spread it to the edges as well. Repeat with another layer of soaked ladyfingers, then the remaining vanilla cream, and finally finish with the remaining banana caramel.

7 Transfer to the refrigerator and let it set for at least 2 hours or preferably overnight before serving. Leftovers will keep, tightly covered, in the refrigerator for up to 5 days.

SAUCES & SECRET WEAPONS

Lemon Dressing
Red Pepper
Olive Oil, page 226
Punchy
Vinaigrette

Lemon Dressing

Makes about ¾ cup

½ cup extra-virgin olive oil
¼ cup fresh lemon juice
1 garlic clove, grated

In a lidded glass jar, combine the olive oil, lemon juice, and garlic. Seal and shake vigorously until emulsified, about 10 seconds. Use as desired, then store in the refrigerator for up to 5 days, being sure to let the dressing return to room temperature and give it a good shake each time before using.

Punchy Vinaigrette

Makes about ½ cup

¼ cup extra-virgin olive oil
¼ cup apple cider vinegar
1 tablespoon Dijon mustard
1 tablespoon honey
⅛ teaspoon kosher salt

In a lidded glass jar, combine the olive oil, cider vinegar, Dijon mustard, honey, and salt. Seal and shake vigorously until emulsified. Use as desired, then store in the refrigerator for up to 5 days, being sure to let the vinaigrette return to room temperature and give it a good shake each time before using.

Red Pepper Olive Oil

Makes 1 cup

1 cup extra-virgin olive oil
1 tablespoon red pepper flakes
1 teaspoon sweet paprika

In a lidded glass jar, combine the olive oil, red pepper flakes, and paprika. Seal and shake well, then let sit at room temperature for 24 hours to infuse. Store at room temperature for up to 3 months.

Romesco Sauce

Makes 2 cups

1 (16-ounce) jar oil-packed roasted red peppers, drained
⅓ cup nuts of your choice, such as cashews, almonds, pecans, or walnuts
1 slice sandwich bread
3 tablespoons sherry vinegar, plus more as needed
3 tablespoons extra-virgin olive oil
2 teaspoons smoked paprika
1 garlic clove, smashed and peeled
1 teaspoon kosher salt, plus more as needed

In a high-powered blender or food processor, combine the roasted peppers, nuts, bread, sherry vinegar, olive oil, smoked paprika, garlic, and salt. Blend on medium speed until smooth, about 2 minutes. Taste and add more salt and vinegar; their flavors should be aggressively powerful. Transfer to an airtight container and store in the refrigerator for up to 5 days.

Honey Mustard Sauce

Makes about ½ cup

- 3 tablespoons whole-grain mustard
- 2 tablespoons Dijon mustard
- 3 tablespoons honey
- 2 tablespoons mayonnaise
- ⅛ teaspoon kosher salt
- ⅛ teaspoon freshly ground black pepper

In a small bowl, whisk together the whole-grain mustard, Dijon, honey, mayonnaise, salt, and pepper. Transfer to an airtight container and store in the refrigerator for up to 5 days.

Chimichurri

Makes 1½ cups

- 3 cups fresh Italian parsley leaves and tender stems
- 5 garlic cloves
- ¼ cup sherry vinegar
- ¼ cup plus 1 tablespoon extra-virgin olive oil
- ¼ teaspoon kosher salt
- ¼ teaspoon red pepper flakes
- 1½ teaspoons honey

1 In a high-powered blender or food processor, combine the parsley, garlic, sherry vinegar, olive oil, salt, and red pepper flakes. Blend on medium-high speed for 1 minute, or until smooth. (If the blades are having a hard time catching the ingredients, reduce the speed to low, add 2 tablespoons cold water, or use the plunger that came with the blender. Then increase the speed and blend until smooth.)

2 Transfer to an airtight container and stir in the honey. Use as desired, or cover and store in the refrigerator for up to 5 days.

Smoked Eggplant Pesto

Makes about 3 cups

- 2 (10-inch) eggplants, halved lengthwise
- ¾ cup extra-virgin olive oil
- 3½ tablespoons fresh lemon juice
- 4 garlic cloves, smashed and peeled (see Note)
- 1 teaspoon kosher salt
- 1 cup packed fresh basil leaves
- 1 bunch Italian parsley, leaves and tender stems (about 2 cups)

1 Position a rack 8 to 10 inches from the broiler heat source and preheat the broiler. Set a wire rack over a baking sheet.

2 Place the eggplant cut-side down on the prepared rack. Broil for about 20 minutes, or until the eggplant skins are deep black and shriveled, the top tan skin is charred, and the aroma has you asking yourself, *Did I overdo this?* (The answer is no—you did not.) Remove from the oven and let rest until cool to the touch, about 15 minutes.

3 Working with one half at a time, hold the eggplant cut-side up, with the bottom of the eggplant facing you. Using a spoon, scoop out the flesh from top to bottom and transfer to a high-powered blender or food processor; discard the charred skins.

4 Add the olive oil, lemon juice, garlic, and salt and blend until smooth, about 1 minute. Add the basil and parsley and pulse until combined and the color of the mixture is tan with specks of green. If using a high-powered blender, you may need to insert the plunger and work it up and down until the herbs catch. Taste and adjust seasoning as needed.

5 Transfer to an airtight container and store in the refrigerator for up to 5 days.

NOTE: To really lean into the spiciness of the raw garlic, consider adding some of the spicy red pepper oil from page 226. To mellow it out, swap the raw garlic for roasted garlic (see page 230).

Smoked Eggplant Pesto

Chimichurri, page 227

Honey Mustard Sauce, page 227

Romesco Sauce, page 226

Sweet & Zingy Fresno Chilies

Makes ¼ cup chilies and ¾ cup pickling liquid

4 Fresno chilies, sliced
½ cup distilled white vinegar
½ cup sugar
1 teaspoon kosher salt

Place the chilies in a lidded heatproof jar that holds at least 8 ounces. In a small saucepan, combine ½ cup water, the vinegar, sugar, and salt and bring to a boil over high heat. Reduce the heat to maintain a simmer and cook, stirring, until the sugar has dissolved, about 30 seconds. Pour the mixture over the chilies. Let cool for 30 minutes, then seal the jar and store in the refrigerator for up to 1 month.

Roasted Garlic

Makes 1 head

1 large garlic head, top ¼ inch cut off
1 tablespoon extra-virgin olive oil
⅛ teaspoon kosher salt
1 teaspoon fresh rosemary leaves, or ¼ teaspoon dried

1 Preheat the oven to 375°F.

2 Tear off a large piece of aluminum foil. Place the garlic on top of the foil, cut-side up. Pour the olive oil over the exposed cloves, then top with the salt and rosemary. Close up the foil around the garlic head, sealing it tightly.

3 Roast for 45 minutes, or until the garlic cloves collapse and ooze when pierced with a fork. Let cool, then squeeze the cloves out of their peels. Use immediately or store in an airtight container in the refrigerator for up to 1 week.

Crispy Prosciutto

Makes 6 or 7 slices

3 ounces sliced prosciutto

1 Preheat the oven to 400°F. Line a baking sheet with parchment paper.

2 Arrange the prosciutto in a single layer on the prepared baking sheet, avoiding overlapping as much as possible. Bake for about 10 minutes, or until the slices have shrunken by about half, their fat has turned amber, and there are wisps of smoke when you open the oven door. Transfer to a paper towel to cool and crisp up, about 10 minutes.

3 Use immediately, or store between paper towels in a resealable plastic bag in the refrigerator for up to 5 days.

Pan-Fried Breadcrumbs

Makes about 1 cup

1 cup panko breadcrumbs
¼ teaspoon granulated garlic
¼ teaspoon freshly ground black pepper
1 tablespoon extra-virgin olive oil

1 In a medium bowl, stir together the panko, granulated garlic, and pepper.

2 In a medium skillet, heat the olive over medium-high heat. When the oil is shimmering, add the panko mixture. Cook, stirring frequently, until golden, about 3 minutes; the breadcrumbs can burn quickly, so keep a close eye on them.

3 Immediately remove the breadcrumbs from the skillet. Use immediately, or let cool then transfer to an airtight container and store at room temperature for up to 1 week.

Cured Egg Yolks

Makes 4 cured yolks

1 cup kosher salt
1 cup sugar
4 large eggs

1 In a medium bowl, whisk together the salt and sugar. Transfer half of the salt to a medium container with a tight-fitting lid. Use one end of an egg to make 4 divots in the curing salt, spacing them apart.

2 Separate the egg yolks from the whites: Crack one egg into a small bowl, then reach in to scoop up the yolk with one hand with your fingers loosely separated. Pass the egg yolk back and forth between your hands until only the yolk remains. Gently place the egg yolk into one of the divots in the curing salt. Repeat with the remaining eggs, reserving the whites for later use (see Note).

3 Add the remaining salt, being sure to cover the yolks completely. Seal the container and place in the refrigerator to cure for 5 days.

4 Preheat the oven to 200°F. Set a wire rack over a baking sheet.

5 Dig out the egg yolks: They should be firm but slightly pliable. Carefully rinse off the salt and set them on the prepared rack. Bake for 20 minutes, until the exteriors are fully dry. Remove from the oven and let cool.

6 Store the yolks, wrapped individually in paper towels, in an airtight container in the refrigerator for up to 2 weeks.

NOTES: If your yolk cracks, it cannot be used in this recipe. Scramble it and make eggs, or use it in as a rich egg wash in the Honey Mustard Tomato Galette on page 79 or the Buttermilk Sage Rolls on page 77. And don't discard the whites—use them in an egg white omelet, or as a lighter egg option in the Stracciatella on page 34.

Acknowledgments

Heather, thank you for helping me so much with this book, testing, shopping, tasting. We did this together. We deserve a bike ride, followed super cheesy shells.

Rachel Dolfi, without you, this book wouldn't exist. You simplified complex thoughts, calmed my nerves on the daily, and told it to me straight when dishes didn't hit the mark. You've got a great palate, passion, and knowledge of cooking that contributed massively to *EAT*. Thank you.

Amanda Englander, you're great at what you do, you know what you want, and those qualities made this book concise and focused—thank you. Lisa Forde, Renée Bollier, Ivy McFadden, and Caroline Hughes, thank you for handling so much, and for making this book the way it is!

Lauren Volo, Monica Pierini, Maeve Sheridan, and Megan Litt: The photos in this book look amazing, the plating, the pairings, the lighting. I had so much fun working with you on all of them, thank you for contributing your gifts to this book, and for listening to me ramble all day, everyday.

Kim Witherspoon, Adam Peck, Max Stubblefield, thank you for getting the word out and landing me with Union Square. Jessica Mileo, thank you for all the edits that made this proposal great.

To my Tastemade family, Larry Fitzgibbon, Jay Holzer, Emily Sweet, Lily Briger. This book wouldn't have been possible without the great TV shows we've made over the years, thank you for continually believing in me, investing in me, and giving me such a great platform to teach and learn about cooking, while making people laugh.

This book wouldn't be in this form without LJ LoMurray, David Sullivan, and Hannah Aufmuth; you're the core of the *Struggle Meals* team and created the foundation that this book stands on. Thank you for years of lifting me up.

Mom, Tess le Moing, Olivia Anderson, Heather, Dr. Diana, Jennifer B, Ashley S, and Monica S. You tested these recipes, told me when things didn't work, and then tested the adjustments. Thank you for the time and effort!

If you've ever watched one of my shows, or if you're a purchaser of this book, thank you. It's incredibly fulfilling to have cooking, recipe creating, and television as my primary career. None of it is possible without you.

Mom and Dad, thank you for your lifelong support and for letting me crash on your couch for two weeks during the photo shoot!

Index

Note: Page numbers in *italic* refer to photographs.

A

anchovies, 19
- Broccoli Rabe Tonnato, *112*, 113
- Seared Caesar, *42*, 43

Anise Biscotti, 214, *215*
apples
- Sheet Pan Pork Chops with Apple & Swiss Chard, 146, *147*

Asparagus & Cheese, *96*, 97
avocado
- Avocado Toast Twins, *68*, 69
- Brekkie, The, *68*, 69
- Italian Cobb Salad with Creamy Gorgonzola Dressing, 40, *41*
- Sleeper, The, *68*, 69

Avocado Toast Twins, *68*, 69

B

Balsamic Strawberry Galette, *81*, *82*, 83
Banana Pull-Apart Bread, *212*, 213
bars
- Chocolate Cherry Brownies, *200*, 201
- Chocolate Peanut Butter Rice Cereal Treats, 206, *207*
- Orange Curd & Pistachio Shortbread Bars, 218, *219*

beef
- Cuban Reuben, 74, *75*
- Meatball Sub, 70, *71*
- Mediterranean Steak, 118, *119*
- Moussaka, 126, *127*
- Spicy Beef Dip, 122, *123*
- Steamed Onion Stroganoff, 54, *55*
- Sweet & Smoky Ribs, *132*, 133
- Thai-Style Beef Salad, *116*, 117
- Vinegar-Braised Short Ribs, *128*, 129

Beermosa, *182*, 183
beets
- Beet Risotto, 58, *59*
- Lentil & Beet Soup, *28*, 29
- Winter Beets with Tarragon Dressing, *44*, *45*

Beet Risotto, 58, *59*
bell peppers
- Bright Black Lentil Salad, *100*, 101
- Cold Bell Pepper Soup, 26, *27*
- Couscous-Stuffed Peppers, 106, *107*
- Spicy Coconut Tofu, *24*, 25

Blackened Flounder with Tarragon Almonds, 172, *173*
black pepper, 20
Bloody Beer, 188, *189*
Blueberry Thyme Shrub, 180, *181*
bouillon paste, 20
bread
- Balsamic Strawberry Galette, *81*, *82*, 83
- Buttermilk Sage Rolls with Whipped Maple Butter, *76*, 77–78
- Everything Soft Pretzel Knots with Mustard Dipping Sauce, *72*, *73*
- French Onion Focaccia, 87–89, *88*
- Garlic Croutons, 37
- Honey Mustard Tomato Galette, 79–80, *81*
- Pan-Fried Breadcrumbs, 231

Brekkie, The, *68*, 69
Bright Black Lentil Salad, *100*, 101
Broccoli Rabe Tonnato, *112*, 113
broccolini
- Roasted Broccolini with Pistachio Parsley Crema, 94, *95*

broth
- Brothy, Spicy Ruffage & Beans, 102, *103*
- Golden Rotisserie Liquid, *38*, 39

Brothy, Spicy Ruffage & Beans, 102, *103*
building flavors, 14
butter, 19
- Spicy Brown Butter Tomatoes, Crispy Arctic Char with, 168, *169*
- Spicy Garlic Butter, Shrimp with, *162*, 163
- Whipped Maple Butter, Buttermilk Sage Rolls with, *76*, 77–78

Buttermilk Sage Rolls with Whipped Maple Butter, *76*, 77–78

C

cake
- Banana Pull-Apart Bread, *212*, 213
- Coconut Poke Cake, 210, *211*
- Ricotta Maple Cheesecake, *208*, 209
- Spiced Sweet Potato Cake with Nutmeg Mascarpone Frosting, *204*, 205

Calabrian chili paste, 20
Caramel Banana Tiracisu, *220*, 221
Carrot Ginger Soup with Garlic Croutons, 36, *37*
carrots
- Carrot Ginger Soup with Garlic Croutons, 36, *37*
- Duck Salad, *148*, 149

Roasted Carrots with Smoky Cashew “Cream,” 98, *99*
cheese, 19, 21. See also specific cheeses
Asparagus & Cheese, *96*, 97
Giant Cheesy Tot, 110, *111*
New York Sicilian Pizza, 84–86, *85*
Ricotta Maple Cheesecake, *208*, 209
Super Cheesy Shells, *64*, 65
Tomato Bisque with Grilled Cheese, *32*, *33*
Chilies, Sweet & Zingy Fresno, 230
citrus, 19
Key Lime Pretzel Icebox Pie, *216*, 217
Lemon Dressing, *224*, 225
Orange Curd & Pistachio Shortbread Bars, 218, *219*
chicken
Curry Chicken Potpie, *144*, 145
Fried Chicken Sandwich, 150, 151
Golden Rotisserie Liquid, *38*, 39
New York Street Cart–Style Chicken & Rice, *140*, 141
Paprika Chicken, *152*, 153
Rosemary Brick Chicken, 138, *139*
Whole Chicken with Bright Spices, Lemon & Potatoes, *136*, 137
Chimichurri, 227, *229*
Chocolate Cherry Brownies, *200*, 201
Chocolate Peanut Butter Rice Cereal Treats, 206, *207*
Choripan, 130, *131*
cocktails
Beermosa, *182*, 183
Bloody Beer, 188, *189*
La Bicicletta, *194*, 195
Moka Martini, 192, *193*
Mountain Toddy, *186*, 187
Necromancer, The, 196, *197*
Nonno’s Martini, *178*, 179
Sour Tequila, 184, *185*
Two-for-One Sangria, *190*, 191
Coconut Poke Cake, 210, *211*
Cold Bell Pepper Soup, 26, *27*
Cold Peanut Noodles, *56*, 57
Couscous-Stuffed Peppers, 106, *107*
Crispy Arctic Char with Spicy Brown Butter Tomatoes, 168, *169*
Crispy Prosciutto, 231
Cuban Reuben, 74, *75*
Cured Egg Yolks, *232*, 233
curry
Curry Chicken Potpie, *144*, 145
Spicy Coconut Tofu, *24*, 25
Curry Chicken Potpie, *144*, 145

D

desserts
Anise Biscotti, 214, *215*
Balsamic Strawberry Galette, *81*, *82*, 83
Banana Pull-Apart Bread, *212*, 213
Caramel Banana Tiracisu, *220*, 221
Chocolate Cherry Brownies, *200*, 201
Chocolate Peanut Butter Rice Cereal Treats, 206, *207*
Coconut Poke Cake, 210, *211*
Key Lime Pretzel Icebox Pie, *216*, 217
Miso Snickerdoodle Ice Cream Sandwiches, 202, *203*
Orange Curd & Pistachio Shortbread Bars, 218, *219*
Ricotta Maple Cheesecake, *208*, 209
Spiced Sweet Potato Cake with Nutmeg Mascarpone Frosting, *204*, 205
dressings
Caesar dressing, 43
Creamy Gorgonzola Dressing, Italian Cobb Salad with, 40, *41*
Lemon Dressing, *224*, 225
Punchy Vinaigrette, *224*, 225
Tarragon Dressing, Winter Beets with, 44, *45*
Tonnato, Broccoli Rabe, *112*, 113
drinks. See also cocktails
Blueberry Thyme Shrub, 180, *181*
Duck Salad, *148*, 149

E

eggplant
Eggplant Fregola, 50, *51*
Moussaka, 126, *127*
Smoked Eggplant Pesto, 228, *229*
Eggplant Fregola, 50, *51*
eggs
Cured Egg Yolks, *232*, 233
Stracciatella, 34, *35*
equipment, 15
essential ingredients, 19–20
Everything Soft Pretzel Knots with Mustard Dipping Sauce, *72*, 73

F

fish
Blackened Flounder with Tarragon Almonds, 172, *173*
Broccoli Rabe Tonnato, *112*, 113
Crispy Arctic Char with Spicy Brown Butter Tomatoes, 168, *169*
Fish Tacos, *170*, 171

fish *(continued)*
Miso Salmon & Chive Rice, 160, *161*
Roasted Branzino with Cilantro Salad, 164, *165*
Roasted Flounder & Potatoes, *174*, 175
Spicy Poached Cod, *166*, 167
Fish Tacos, *170*, 171
French Onion Focaccia, 87–89, *88*
Fried Chicken Sandwich, 150, 151

G

garlic, 19
Garlic Croutons, 37
Garlic Turkey Meatloaf, 154, *155*
granulated, 20
Garlic Croutons, 37
Garlic Turkey Meatloaf, 154, *155*
Giant Cheesy Tot, 110, *111*
ginger, 19
Carrot Ginger Soup with Garlic Croutons, 36, *37*
Golden Rotisserie Liquid, *38*, 39
Grilled Calamari Salad, *158*, 159
Grilled Cheese, Tomato Bisque with, *32*, 33

H

Honey Mustard Sauce, 227, *229*
Honey Mustard Tomato Galette, 79–80, *81*

I

In-Your-Face Tomato Salad, *108*, 109
Italian Cobb Salad with Creamy Gorgonzola Dressing, 40, *41*

K

Key Lime Pretzel Icebox Pie, *216*, 217
knives, 16–17

L

La Bicicletta, *194*, 195
lamb
Lamb Meatballs with Garlicky Yogurt, *120*, 121
Spiced Roasted Lamb & Zhoug Orzo, *124*, 125
Lamb Meatballs with Garlicky Yogurt, *120*, 121
Lemon Dressing, *224*, 225
Lentil & Beet Soup, *28*, 29
lentils
Bright Black Lentil Salad, *100*, 101
Lentil & Beet Soup, *28*, 29
Love Letter to Mozzarella, A, 21

M

measurements, 13–14
Meatball Sub, 70, *71*
Mediterranean Steak, 118, *119*
Miso Salmon & Chive Rice, 160, *161*
Miso Snickerdoodle Ice Cream Sandwiches, 202, *203*
Moka Martini, 192, *193*
Mountain Toddy, *186*, 187
Moussaka, 126, *127*
mozzarella, 21
Love Letter to Mozzarella, A, 21
New York Sicilian Pizza, 84–86, *85*
Pasta with Mozzarella, *52*, 53
Super Cheesy Shells, *64*, 65
mustard, 20

N

Necromancer, The, 196, *197*
neutral oil, 20
New York Sicilian Pizza, 84–86, *85*
New York Street Cart-Style Chicken & Rice, *140*, 141
Nonno's Martini, *178*, 179

O

olive oil, 20
onion, 19
French Onion Focaccia, 87–89, *88*
Steamed Onion Stroganoff, *54*, *55*
Orange Curd & Pistachio Shortbread Bars, 218, *219*

P

Pan-Fried Breadcrumbs, 231
Paprika Chicken, *152*, 153
Parmigiano Reggiano, 19
pasta
Cold Peanut Noodles, *56*, 57
Eggplant Fregola, 50, *51*
Pasta with Mozzarella, *52*, 53
Spicy Rigatoni with Fennel Sausage Ragù, *48*, 49
Steamed Onion Stroganoff, *54*, *55*
Summer Pasta, 62, *63*
Super Cheesy Shells, *64*, 65
Super Garlic Spaghetti, *60*, 61
Pasta with Mozzarella, *52*, 53
Pea Vichyssoise, 30, *31*
Pecorino Romano, 19
pie
Key Lime Pretzel Icebox Pie, *216*, 217
Pizza, New York Sicilian, 84–86, 85
pork
Choripan, 130, *131*

Meatball Sub, 70, *71*
Pork Cutlet with Fennel Slaw, 142, *143*
Sheet Pan Pork Chops with Apple & Swiss Chard, 146, *147*
Spicy Rigatoni with Fennel Sausage Ragù, *48*, 49
Pork Cutlet with Fennel Slaw, 142, *143*
potatoes
Giant Cheesy Tot, 110, *111*
mashed potatoes and celery root, 129
Pea Vichyssoise, 30, *31*
Roasted Baby Potatoes with Zingy Romesco Sauce, *104*, 105
Roasted Flounder & Potatoes, *174*, 175
Whole Chicken with Bright Spices, Lemon & Potatoes, *136*, 137
poultry
Curry Chicken Potpie, *144*, 145
Duck Salad, *148*, 149
Fried Chicken Sandwich, 150, 151
Garlic Turkey Meatloaf, 154, *155*
New York Street Cart-Style Chicken & Rice, *140*, 141
Paprika Chicken, *152*, 153
Rosemary Brick Chicken, 138, *139*
Whole Chicken with Bright Spices, Lemon & Potatoes, *136*, 137
Punchy Vinaigrette, *224*, 225

R

Red Pepper Olive Oil, *224*, 226
rice
Beet Risotto, 58, *59*
Miso Salmon & Chive Rice, 160, *161*
New York Street Cart-Style Chicken & Rice, *140*, 141
Paprika Chicken, *152*, 153
toasted rice powder, 117
rice noodles
Spicy Coconut Tofu, *24*, 25
Ricotta Maple Cheesecake, *208*, 209
Roasted Baby Potatoes with Zingy Romesco Sauce, *104*, 105
Roasted Branzino with Cilantro Salad, 164, *165*
Roasted Broccolini with Pistachio Parsley Crema, 94, *95*
Roasted Carrots with Smoky Cashew "Cream," 98, *99*
Roasted Flounder & Potatoes, *174*, 175
Roasted Garlic, 230
Romesco Sauce, 226, *229*
Rosemary Brick Chicken, 138, *139*

S

salads
Duck Salad, *148*, 149
Italian Cobb Salad with Creamy Gorgonzola Dressing, 40, *41*
Seared Caesar, *42*, 43
Thai-Style Beef Salad, *116*, 117
Winter Beets with Tarragon Dressing, *44*, *45*
salt, 14, 19–20
sandwiches
Avocado Toast Twins, *68*, 69
Brekkie, The, *68*, 69
Cuban Reuben, 74, *75*
Grilled Cheese, Tomato Bisque with, *32*, 33
Meatball Sub, 70, *71*
Sleeper, The, *68*, 69
sauces
Chimichurri, 227, *229*
Honey Mustard Sauce, 227, *229*
Pineapple BBQ Sauce, 133
Red Pepper Olive Oil, *224*, 226
Romesco Sauce, 226, *229*
Smoked Eggplant Pesto, 228, *229*
seafood
Blackened Flounder with Tarragon Almonds, 172, *173*
Broccoli Rabe Tonnato, *112*, 113
Crispy Arctic Char with Spicy Brown Butter Tomatoes, 168, *169*
Fish Tacos, *170*, 171
Grilled Calamari Salad, *158*, 159
Miso Salmon & Chive Rice, 160, *161*
Roasted Branzino with Cilantro Salad, 164, *165*
Roasted Flounder & Potatoes, *174*, 175
Shrimp with Spicy Garlic Butter, *162*, 163
Spicy Poached Cod, *166*, 167
Seared Caesar, *42*, 43
Sheet Pan Pork Chops with Apple & Swiss Chard, 146, *147*
Shrimp with Spicy Garlic Butter, *162*, 163
Sleeper, The, *68*, 69
Smoked Eggplant Pesto, 228, *229*
soups
Carrot Ginger Soup with Garlic Croutons, 36, *37*
Cold Bell Pepper Soup, 26, *27*
Golden Rotisserie Liquid, *38*, 39
Lentil & Beet Soup, *28*, 29
Pea Vichyssoise, 30, *31*
Spicy Coconut Tofu, *24*, 25
Stracciatella, 34, *35*
Tomato Bisque with Grilled Cheese, *32*, 33
Sour Tequila, 184, *185*

Spiced Roasted Lamb & Zhoug Orzo, *124*, 125
Spiced Sweet Potato Cake with Nutmeg Mascarpone Frosting, *204*, 205
spices, 19
Spicy Beef Dip, 122, *123*
Spicy Coconut Tofu, *24*, 25
Spicy Poached Cod, *166*, 167
Spicy Rigatoni with Fennel Sausage Ragù, *48*, 49
squid
  Grilled Calamari Salad, *158*, 159
Steamed Onion Stroganoff, 54, *55*
Stracciatella, 34, *35*
Summer Pasta, 62, *63*
Summer Zucchini Sauté, *92*, 93
Super Cheesy Shells, *64*, 65
Super Garlic Spaghetti, *60*, 61
Sweet & Smoky Ribs, *132*, 133
Sweet & Zingy Fresno Chilies, 230

T

Thai-Style Beef Salad, *116*, 117
Tofu, Spicy Coconut, *24*, 25
Tomato Bisque with Grilled Cheese, *32*, 33
tomatoes
  Honey Mustard Tomato Galette, 79–80, *81*
  In-Your-Face Tomato Salad, *108*, 109
  Italian Cobb Salad with Creamy Gorgonzola Dressing, 40, *41*
  Pasta with Mozzarella, *52*, 53
  Spicy Brown Butter Tomatoes, Crispy Arctic Char with, 168, *169*
  Spicy Poached Cod, *166*, 167
  Summer Pasta, 62, *63*
  Summer Zucchini Sauté, *92*, 93
  Tomato Bisque with Grilled Cheese, *32*, 33
tuna
  Broccoli Rabe Tonnato, *112*, 113
turkey
  Garlic Turkey Meatloaf, 154, *155*
Two-for-One Sangria, *190*, 191

V

vegetables. See also specific vegetables
  Asparagus & Cheese, *96*, 97
  Beet Risotto, 58, *59*
  Brekkie, The, *68*, 69
  Broccoli Rabe Tonnato, *112*, 113
  Brothy, Spicy Ruffage & Beans, 102, *103*
  Carrot Ginger Soup with Garlic Croutons, 36, *37*
  Cold Bell Pepper Soup, 26, *27*
  Couscous-Stuffed Peppers, 106, *107*
  Eggplant Fregola, 50, *51*
  Giant Cheesy Tot, 110, *111*
  In-Your-Face Tomato Salad, *108*, 109
  Pea Vichyssoise, 30, *31*
  Roasted Baby Potatoes with Zingy Romesco Sauce, *104*, 105
  Roasted Broccolini with Pistachio Parsley Crema, *94*, *95*
  Roasted Carrots with Smoky Cashew "Cream," 98, *99*
  Roasted Garlic, 230
  Romesco Sauce, 226, *229*
  Seared Caesar, *42*, 43
  Sleeper, The, *68*, 69
  Smoked Eggplant Pesto, 228, *229*
  Steamed Onion Stroganoff, 54, *55*
  Summer Pasta, 62, *63*
  Summer Zucchini Sauté, *92*, 93
  Super Garlic Spaghetti, *60*, 61
  Sweet & Zingy Fresno Chilies, 230
  Tomato Bisque with Grilled Cheese, *32*, 33
  Winter Beets with Tarragon Dressing, *44*, *45*
vinegar, 20
Vinegar-Braised Short Ribs, *128*, 129

W

white wine, 20
Whole Chicken with Bright Spices, Lemon & Potatoes, *136*, 137
Winter Beets with Tarragon Dressing, *44*, *45*

Z

zucchini
  Summer Pasta, 62, *63*
  Summer Zucchini Sauté, *92*, 93